The college football rivalry
between Michigan and Ohio State
will always be known as
The Game.

THE TEN YEAR WAR
Ten Classic Games
Between Bo and Woody

BY

JOEL PENNINGTON

Published by Ulyssian Publications, an imprint of Pine Orchard, Inc.
Visit us on the internet at www.pineorchard.com.
Printed in Canada.

http://www.thetenyearwar.com/

ISBN 1-930580-78-9
EAN 978-1930580-78-7
Library of Congress Control Number 2005905801

Contents

Acknowledgments

WHEN I FIRST BEGAN THIS BOOK, I knew that I was going to need the support of the people who played in and coached these games. Almost without exception, everyone I spoke with was not only gracious enough to grant me some of their time, but they were also quick to offer encouragement and advice. Woody and Bo both preached the concept of "paying forward," and their players have certainly embraced that philosophy. Whether from Ohio State or Michigan, I'm very grateful to every one of them.

Without the blessing and assistance of Bo Schembechler, this book would have been an even greater challenge. Thanks, coach. Your recollection of events was unbelievable, and I don't know what I would have done without your help finding your former players. The men who played for you speak of you in reverent terms; and after spending some time with you, I certainly understand why. I hope this book does justice to the great games you and Woody had.

If there is a better college football historian than Jack Park, I'd be shocked. His knowledge, research, and passion for the sport have set a high standard for everyone else to follow. I literally don't have the words to express my gratitude for all the advice and assistance Jack has given me. His wisdom has guided me through the formation of this book and I am indebted to him. Getting to know him has been one of the bonuses of this project. I'm proud to call Jack Park my friend.

Mary Passink at the University of Michigan football office was also a tremendous help. Her kindness and patience after my many calls to Bo were greatly appreciated. I hope I am as efficient and courteous in my dealings with people as she is.

Many thanks to Kevin Kempton at Kemtech Design for his excellent work on the book's website as well as the cover art. I can't recommend his work highly enough.

I would also like to thank Carolyn Gravelle and her staff at Pine Orchard. Her recommendations and assistance smoothed some bumps along the way. She has been wonderful to work with and I look forward to working with Pine Orchard again.

If anyone deserves my gratitude, it's my lovely wife Libbi. Your faith in me and your patience have enabled me to fulfill a lifetime dream. This book would not have been possible without your constant encouragement and love. I dedicate it to you and the girls.

Finally, I want to thank God. Whatever successes I have are due to Him; my failures are my own.

I want to thank those who gave interviews for this book:

MICHIGAN	OHIO STATE
Bo Schembechler	Earle Bruce
Gary Moeller	George Chaump
Jerry Hanlon	Ed Ferkany
Don Canham	
John Anderson	Ernie Andria
Gordon Bell	Brian Baschnagel
Dave Brown	Tom Campana
Gil Chapman	Dave Cheney
Thom Darden	Tom Cousineau
Russell Davis	Van DeCree
Tim Davis	Rick Galbos
Bill Dufek	Randy Gradishar
Dennis Franklin	Archie Griffin
Curtis Greer	Luther Henson
Mike Jolly	John Hicks
Mike Lantry	Rex Kern
Rick Leach	Tom Klaban
Rob Lytle	Elmer Lippert
Reggie McKenzie	Jeff Logan
Don Moorhead	Jim Otis
Guy Murdock	Jim Pacenta
Barry Pierson	Jim Savoca
Ed Shuttlesworth	Tom Skladany

OTHERS

Wayne Duke
Jerry Markbreit
Jack Park

Preface

ALTHOUGH THE THOUGHT OF WRITING A BOOK about the ten games between Bo and Woody had been in my mind for several years, it wasn't until the 100th Michigan-Ohio State game in 2003 that I decided to stop thinking about it and start doing it. Each year, around the week of "The Game," all the great moments in the history of the rivalry are told and re-told, and this was especially true when the two old rivals met for the 100th time in 2003.

Of course, when discussing the rivalry between Michigan and Ohio State, one period of time is always mentioned first: The Ten Year War.

Even though those ten games are always mentioned as the golden age of the rivalry, I never felt that they had been covered in enough detail. As I was sitting in Michigan Stadium on November 22, 2003, I decided that I would set out to write this book. I thought that it would be a lot of work, but I also thought that it would be an interesting journey. I was more than correct on both counts.

I knew that the story of these games would best be told by the people who participated in them, and the cooperation I received from the players and coaches from both programs was unbelievable. The class and graciousness that these men displayed are a tribute not only to them, but also to Woody and Bo. To be able to listen to the stories of the people who were part of these classic games was an honor. I hope I have done them justice in this book.

These games are fascinating on several levels. Not only were they almost always for the Big Ten title, the Rose Bowl, and a shot at the National Championship, they were the personal battles of two giants who happened to be great friends. The story is almost like something out of a Hollywood script. Woody coached Bo at Miami of Ohio, hired him as an assistant at Ohio State, and then competed against him in the greatest rivalry in all of sports.

The Ten Year War had it all. There were great players, great coaches, big plays, controversy, goal line stands, upsets, crunching defense, dramatic kicks, sideline eruptions, huge wins, bitter defeats, great comebacks, and much more. It's my desire that you enjoy reading this book as much as I did writing it.

—Joel Pennington
2005

THE TEN YEAR WAR

Wayne Woodrow
and
Glenn Edward

L ATE ONE NIGHT IN THE SPRING 1960, Wayne Woodrow Hayes and Glenn Edward Schembechler were in the football offices at Ohio State watching game film. There was a certain play that needed work, and the head coach and his assistant just couldn't agree about which blocking technique should be used. Both were experts at the nuances of offensive line play, and both were stubborn, strong-willed men who had very firm ideas about their opinions.

After going back and forth for a while, Woody had finally had enough. He picked up a chair and threw it across the room in the general direction of Bo. Never one to back down, Bo picked the chair off the floor and tossed it back towards Woody.

"You're fired!" Woody screamed. "Get out of my sight."

Bo stormed out the room and went into the men's room to splash some water on his now very red face. "I was staring into the mirror thinking about how I had just been fired," Bo explains. "A few minutes later, Woody comes walking in. I don't even think he was specifically looking for me. He just needed to use the men's room. He said, 'Okay, let's get back to work now,' and that was it. We went back in and put the room back together and finished breaking down the film. We had both said our piece. It was time to get back to business. I would have gone back in, even if he hadn't told me to. I wouldn't have let something as trivial as getting fired get in the way of football."

In March of 1987, Bo Schembechler was being honored at a banquet in Dayton, Ohio, and Woody Hayes was scheduled to be the keynote speaker. When Bo arrived at the hall, he was taken aback at how ill and weak Woody appeared. Bo found the ceremony's organizers and told them that he was livid that they had dragged an obviously ailing Woody to this event. They told Bo that they tried to convince Woody not to come, but that he had insisted on honoring his friend.

"It hurt me to see him like that. But when he got up to speak, he was magical," Bo remembers. "He was as mesmerizing as he always was and spoke for a long time. Standing behind that podium while speaking for that long had to take a lot out of him. Even though it was obvious he wasn't well, he wanted to pay tribute to me. That's how he was. The next day, he died."

These stories give a small glimpse into a very complex relationship. Bo played for Woody, coached with Woody, and coached against Woody. But the mutual respect and admiration they had for one another bridged all those different circumstances. And the tenacious competition they displayed during the ten games they coached against each other only deepened those feelings. The respect these two had for one another filtered down to their respective teams.

Ohio State was known as "The Graveyard of Coaches" when Woody Hayes took over. Of the previous fifteen Buckeye coaches, only Francis Schmidt had a winning record against the hated Wolverines. Hayes' predecessor, Wes Fesler, had gone 0-3-1 against Michigan, including a 9-3 loss in the famous Snow Bowl game of 1950. A few weeks after that defeat, Fesler resigned as head coach citing the effects of the job was having on his health.

With Fesler's departure, the Ohio State administration was looking for someone who could beat Michigan and would have the intestinal fortitude to withstand the intense pressure that any Buckeye coach would be sure to encounter. When they hired Woody Hayes from Miami of Ohio, they had found the man who would fulfill both of those requirements and then some.

After serving as a naval officer in the Second World War, Woody had been a successful head coach at Denison and then at Miami. His success at those schools, coupled with his intense will to win, made him an attractive candidate to take over the head job at Ohio State.

The selection committee initially offered the job to Missouri coach Don Faurot, and he accepted. But after a few days, Faurot reconsidered and decided to remain at Missouri. It was then that the position was offered to Woody, and the rest is history.

Interestingly, one of the other top candidates was Cincinnati coach Sid Gillman. Woody's Miami team had beaten Gillman 28-0 on the same day that the famous Snow Bowl was played. One of the starters on that Miami team was an offensive lineman named Bo Schembechler.

Woody Hayes endured a few rocky moments as he built the Ohio State program in his image the first few seasons. He started out 1-2 against Michigan and had a mediocre 16-9-2 record heading into the 1954 season. That year, Ohio State went 10-0 and beat USC in the Rose Bowl to capture the National Championship. The Buckeyes went on to capture the Big Ten title again in 1955, and won both the Big Ten and National Championship in 1957.

In 1961, Ohio State went 8-0-1 and beat Michigan 50-20 to clinch a trip to the Rose Bowl. But the Ohio State faculty council voted to turn down the invitation because they felt that football was getting too much emphasis and was a detriment to the goals of the university. When Woody received the news, he was in

Cleveland getting ready to speak at an alumni dinner. Before giving his speech, Woody walked around the streets of Cleveland allowing his temper to subside.

Who was at his side step by step? A young assistant coach named Bo Schembechler.

That controversial vote hindered Woody's recruiting efforts, and the Ohio State program endured several seasons of mediocre records as a result. By 1968, the Buckeyes had gone seven years without winning the Big Ten title. But Hayes' best years lay ahead of him. Woody had brought in one of the best classes in college football history in 1967, and they would propel the program to the National Championship in 1968 and a 50-14 whitewashing of highly ranked Michigan.

The Ohio State football program became a reflection of the head coach. Hayes' strict adherence to discipline and fundamental, physical football filtered down to his players. The Buckeyes beat teams by out-hitting, outworking, and out-executing them. Woody was also one of the best recruiters in the country, and he knew how to get the most out of the talent he stockpiled.

"Woody understood what made each player tick," defensive end Van DeCree explains. "He knew how to motivate. And once he had all that talent motivated, very few teams could stand up to us. People might stay close for one or two quarters. But after that, our depth and physical style of play just overwhelmed them. We might be up 14-7 at halftime and end up winning 45-10. He had it down to a science."

As the Ten Year War approached, Woody had completely changed the course of the rivalry. Before his arrival, Ohio State was 12-32-3 against the Wolverines. In his first 18 seasons, Woody had compiled a 12-6 record against "that team up north" and had administered two of the worst beatings in the history of Michigan football in 1961 and 1968. He was reaching the pinnacle of his power, and he had positioned his program to continue to be one of the nation's best for the next decade.

While Ohio State had become a college football superpower under the direction of Woody Hayes, Michigan had endured two decades of mediocrity. After winning the Big Ten title in the 1950 Snow Bowl game against Ohio State, the Wolverines managed only one more title in the following 18 seasons. When Don Canham was hired as Michigan's new athletic director in 1968, he knew that one of his biggest challenges would be to rebuild the once proud football program.

"When I took over as head of the athletic department in 1968, Bump Elliott and I agreed that it would be his last season," Canham explained. "He wanted to get into athletic administration, and he became Michigan's first associate athletic director. So I knew that one of my biggest jobs that first year would be to hire a new football coach after the 1968 season. I knew this would be a vital decision because without a successful football program, your stadium is half-empty and revenues are going to suffer."

Canham's first choice as new coach wasn't Bo. It was Joe Paterno.

"I actually offered the job to Paterno and he considered taking it," Canham recalled. "But he had only recently taken over at Penn State and didn't want to leave. After that, whenever I would talk to football people, the name of a young coach at Miami of Ohio would keep coming up. When I interviewed Bo, it was obvious he was the man for the job. He had all the credentials I was looking for. He was a Midwest guy, which was essential for recruiting. He had the pedigree by coaching for Woody Hayes and Ara Parseghian, and he was incredibly intense. He didn't even ask how much money he would make until he had accepted the job."

Bo had played for Woody Hayes at Miami of Ohio and the two had become close. Upon graduation, Bo was a graduate assistant for Woody at Ohio State in 1951. From there, Bo went on to serve as an assistant to Doyt Perry at Bowling Green and Ara Parseghian at Northwestern. In 1958, his mentor called to offer him a position at Ohio State. Bo accepted and worked for Woody for five seasons. It was during this time that Bo and Woody forged their lifelong friendship, and Bo soaked up many of Woody's football philosophies.

"When I was offered the head coaching job at Miami of Ohio, Woody told me I couldn't go," Bo recalls. "He said that he would only coach for a few more seasons, and then I would take over at Ohio State. Well, I really wanted the Ohio State job. But I knew that Woody wasn't going anywhere soon, and that even when he did, he wouldn't be able to just name his successor. So I went to talk to Dick Larkins, the Ohio State athletic director, and told him that Miami had offered me the job. He just said, 'You'd better win.' He knew that I wanted the Ohio State job and that this might be an opportunity for me to prove myself. But things didn't quite work out that way."

After winning two MAC titles at Miami, Don Canham came calling with an offer to take over the Michigan program. Bo remembers not taking very long to decide. "I jumped at the opportunity. I knew that with Michigan's tradition, we could really build something special."

When Bo arrived in Ann Arbor in December of 1968, he was surprised at how bad the facilities were. "We didn't even have lockers for our coaching staff. We hung our clothes on nails that were nailed into a wood plank on the wall. I knew that we were going to have to make changes, not just in the facilities, but in the attitudes surrounding the program. Things were going to be different."

Bo had learned many things from Woody, and he was determined to mold the Michigan program in a similar manner to what he had seen Woody do at Ohio State. Bo had two fundamental goals when it came to rebuilding Michigan football:

"We built our program on the basic principle of tough, aggressive football. And we built it with the goal of beating Ohio State."

"I think Woody knew things were going to change when Bo got the Michigan job," Earle Bruce explains. "He knew that this would become a personal rivalry as much as a college football rivalry. The competition would now extend from the field to the recruiting trail. Bo understood the Ohio State program from the inside, and Woody knew he was going to have his hands full from then on. He knew that the rivalry would get ratcheted up a notch."

With Woody firmly entrenched in Columbus and Bo taking over in Ann Arbor, there was a perfect storm of circumstances that sent these two rival programs onto a collision course with each other. The rivalry had always been huge, but these two men would take it to heights that had never been reached before.

The Ten Year War was under way.

THE GAME 1969

To borrow a famous line from Charles Dickens: "It was the best of times, it was the worst of times." And your opinion of this tale of two cities, Ann Arbor and Columbus, depends on whether your loyalty lies with Michigan or Ohio State. If you love the Buckeyes, then November 22, 1969, was a black Saturday that snatched away a certain national championship and wrecked what was supposed to be the coronation of the greatest college football team of all time. If you love Michigan, it was a glorious day that signaled the awakening of a sleeping giant and purged the shame from the previous year.

Either way, it was the first shot fired in the Ten Year War. And not only was the 1969 Michigan-Ohio State game one of the biggest upsets in the history of college football, it set the table for every edition of "The Game" to follow. As huge as the rivalry had always been, after 1969 it would never be the same again.

The seeds of the 1969 game had been sown on the grass field of Ohio Stadium in 1968. What was supposed to be a classic match-up between two top-five teams turned into a Buckeye blitzkrieg as #2 Ohio State crushed and humiliated #4 Michigan 50-14 on their way to the National Championship. Leading just 21-14 at halftime, Ohio State demolished the Wolverines in the second half; and as the margin increased, the Buckeyes just kept pouring it on. With under a minute and a half remaining and the score at 44-14, the Ohio State reserves were at the Michigan 2 yard line. Woody Hayes allowed starting fullback Jim Otis to re-enter the game, and Otis hammered into the end zone for his fourth touchdown of the day.

If that wasn't bad enough, with the score now 50-14, Ohio State lined up for a two-point conversion. The pass failed, but the Michigan players were livid at what seemed to be an attempt to embarrass them. With under a minute left, Michigan quarterback Don Moorhead was taken out of bounds and then the fists started flying. Order was quickly restored, but the hard feelings only intensified.

There has been much speculation on whether Hayes ordered the two-point conversion or whether it was the product of disorganization on the field by the celebrating Ohio State players. The story that is most famous is that when asked after the game by a reporter why he went for two, Woody answered, "Because I couldn't go for three!"

According to players and coaches though, that is an urban myth. "I was right there," said assistant coach George Chaump, "and I can tell you it wasn't Woody's decision to go for two. There was so much confusion after we had scored to go ahead 50-14 that the players couldn't get lined up for an extra point attempt. The stuff about I-couldn't-go-for-three just made for a good story."

Even if the two-point try hadn't been Hayes' call, putting Jim Otis back into the game to score the final touchdown certainly was. Woody was no stranger to irritating Michigan if the opportunity presented itself.

Interestingly, Woody had called for a two-point conversion at the end of the 1961 Michigan-Ohio State game, and the Buckeyes got it to make the final score 50-20. A young Ohio State assistant coach named Bo Schembechler was coaching from the press box that day. "Some people blame me for that 1961 call," Bo remembers with a laugh. "But that one was all on Woody. Shoot, he turned off the headset I was talking to him on about midway through the fourth quarter. I just sat and watched the game the final five minutes or so."

Regardless of the circumstances of the final few minutes of the 1968 game, the Michigan players were humiliated and angry. Inside the cramped visitors' locker room in Ohio Stadium, the celebration outside rang loudly.

"We heard the crowd celebrating outside," Don Moorhead remembers. "We told each other to remember the feeling we had at that moment because we would use it to fuel our preparation in the off-season. We planned on beating Ohio State the next year."

Worrying about teams who wanted revenge wasn't something the 1969 Ohio State Buckeyes spent their time doing. They were too busy destroying everyone and everything in their path. At that time, no other team in modern Big Ten history had been as dominant. The "Super Sophomores" of the 1968 National Championship team were now juniors and they were the scourge of college football.

After the Buckeyes crushed Wisconsin 62-7, Badger coach John Coatta was quoted as saying, "I was about to go see if all those Ohio State players had a big S on their chests."

The scores were gaudy as no team came within four touchdowns of the Buckeyes, and they scored over 40 points six times in their first eight games. Since most of the games were essentially over before halftime, the Ohio State starters rarely played more than a series or two in the second half, or the margins would have been even greater.

Junior quarterback Rex Kern was a great passer and was the leader of the offense. Kern possessed tremendous athletic ability and was a master at running the option and confusing defenses with his ball handling skills. Kern's backup was Ron Maciejowski, who would have started for most other teams, and there wasn't much of a drop off when he entered the game. There was an embarrassment of talent in the backfield. Senior Jim

Otis was one of the best fullbacks that Ohio State ever produced and he shared time with future NFL star John Brockington. Leo Hayden, Larry Zelina, and Ray Gillian filled out the star-studded backfield, and they all got plenty of carries.

The offensive line had lost the two star tackles from 1968 in Rufus Mayes and Dave Foley, but Dave Cheney and Charles Hutchison had filled their large shoes very well. Brian Donovan was named All Conference on the interior of the offensive line, and future All-American Tom Deleone was starting at center by late in the year. Jan White, Bruce Jankowski, and Dick Kuhn combined to give Ohio State a very deep set of pass catchers. All this incredible talent averaged 46.4 points and 320 rushing yards per game heading into the Michigan contest.

While the offense was racking up yards and points, the defense was punishing people as seven defensive players were named first team All-Big Ten. All-Everything middle guard Jim Stillwagon destroyed the middle of opponent's offenses. Mark Debevc, Paul Schmidlin, David Whitfield, and Bill Urbanik filled out the defensive line while Doug Adams, Phil Strickland, and Stan White formed a very good linebacking corps. The secondary was by far the best in the country with two All-Americans in Jack Tatum and Ted Provost, and two other great players in Tim Anderson and Mike Sensibaugh. Tatum was the most feared defensive player in the country and he would earn the title "Assassin" during his NFL career.

Almost to a man, the players from this team believe that the 1969 team was better than the 1968 team that had beaten USC in the Rose Bowl to win the National Championship.

"Oh, there's no doubt in my mind that the 1969 team was the best team I played on at Ohio State," remembers Jim Otis. "Nobody could touch us."

Rex Kern agrees. "In my opinion, the 1969 team had the best talent in Ohio State football history. In 1968, we were perfect. We won every game we played in 1968, while in 1969 we lost one which cost us another National Championship! I think the 1969 team had more talent overall."

The national press had started singing their praises as well. Many writers mentioned that Ohio State was good enough to play most NFL teams and they were being hailed as the greatest team in college football team in history. Woody Hayes had always believed that praise made you soft and left you vulnerable. He preached that the more you basked in the sunshine, the less prepared you were if there were to be a storm. As the praise and accolades continued to pour into Columbus, Ohio, it's doubtful that even Woody could see the gathering storm clouds.

While Ohio State was the class of college football, Michigan was a program in transition. Bo Schembechler's first year wasn't without some acute growing pains. After big wins in their first two games, Michigan was beaten soundly at home by a good Missouri team. Two weeks later, the Wolverines lost at East Lansing to Michigan State. With their record at 3-2 and the team racked with injuries, Michigan had to travel to Minnesota the following week.

At the half, the Gophers led 9-7 and Bo could feel that his depleted team faced a crucial moment in their season. Instead of laying into his players at halftime, Bo calmly told them that another loss would kill their championship hopes. But he reassured them that their goals were still within reach. Schembechler's calm demeanor motivated a banged-up and beleaguered team as they totally dominated the second half, winning the game 35-9.

That was the turning point. The rejuvenated Wolverines demolished their next three opponents by an aggregate score of 143-13. The Michigan offense was sixth in the country in scoring and averaged 36.1 points per game. Junior quarterback Don Moorhead was a good passer and runner, and was complemented by a solid backfield. Garvie Craw and John Gabler took most of the snaps at fullback and wingback while Glenn Doughty and Billy Taylor formed a solid tandem at tailback. The offensive line was very good when healthy and was anchored by Dick Caldarazzo, Dan Dierdorf, Jack Harping, Bob Baumgartner, and Guy Murdock. Several other offensive linemen contributed as injuries forced the coaching staff to juggle the lineup. When Michigan chose to pass, Moorhead usually looked for All-American tight end and team captain Jim Mandich.

The Michigan defense was solid but not spectacular. Undersized middle guard Henry Hill and defensive tackle Pete Newell clogged up the middle while linebackers Marty Huff and Mike Taylor cleaned up behind them. Safety Tom Curtis had six interceptions for the year and an amazing 23 in his career heading into the Ohio State game. Curtis teamed with Brian Healey, Thom Darden, and Barry Pierson to form a very good secondary.

As the season unfolded, both teams seemed to be hitting their peak leading up to "The Game." But the summit at Ohio State was higher than any other in college football. They were simply laying waste to their opposition.

The week before the Michigan game, Ohio State faced their biggest challenge to date against tenth-ranked Purdue. After dismantling the Boilermakers 42-14, President Richard Nixon called to congratulate his friend Woody Hayes on the great victory.

Shell-shocked Purdue coach Jack Mollenkopf had nothing but the highest praise for the Buckeyes. "They've got it all. There's no defense better unless it's the Minnesota Vikings."

While Ohio State was burying Purdue, Michigan was at Iowa City where they dismantled the Hawkeyes 51-6. The day before the game, Bo surprised his team by telling them that they would beat Iowa on Saturday, then beat Ohio State the following week, and go to the Rose Bowl.

After beating Iowa, the fired-up Wolverines massed in the Kinnick Stadium locker room and went berserk. "You can ask anyone who was in that locker room that day," Gary Moeller recalls. "Those players were screaming and yelling and started chanting 'beat the Bucks, beat the Bucks' so loud that I thought the walls were going to cave in. I'm not exaggerating when I say that this went on for ten minutes. As assistants, we wanted to calm them down. But Bo just let them go. I wanted to play Ohio State right then and there. I knew we had a great shot to beat them. I remember Bo telling Jerry Hanlon that Ohio State had better be ready because we were coming after them."

Regardless of what the Michigan staff and players believed, nobody else was giving the Wolverines a chance against the mighty Buckeyes. Since the Big Ten's no-repeat rule was in place, Ohio State wouldn't be going to the Rose Bowl. After the formality of beating Michigan was accomplished, the Buckeyes would be awarded their second consecutive National Championship and would take their place in history as college football's greatest team.

Even though the game was at Ann Arbor, the odds makers had Ohio State as a 15- point favorite. When asked who he thought would win the game, Purdue coach Jack Mollenkopf didn't mince words: "I don't think Michigan has a chance against them." That opinion was shared by almost everyone outside of Ann Arbor.

The week of the game, it was difficult to be around the Michigan practice facilities without noticing the number 50. Not that any Michigan player needed to be reminded, but 50-14 was the final score of the 1968 game and Bo wanted to make sure everyone remembered.

Offensive lineman Guy Murdock remembers seeing the number 50 everywhere he looked. "Bo put 50's all over the place. We had them on the walls and even on the shower curtains. He even put the entire scout team in a number 50 jersey. Usually, your scout players wear numbers that correspond to the opposing player they are emulating. But not that week. They were all number 50."

When Saturday finally arrived, Michigan Stadium was filled to capacity. Sell-out crowds weren't an every-game occurrence at Michigan at that time. It would take a few more years of Don Canham's marketing and Bo Schembechler's winning until Michigan Stadium was filled every week. On Monday of this week, Canham personally delivered 22,000 tickets to the Ohio State ticket office. Almost one-third of the crowd would be cheering for the Buckeyes.

The Michigan fans that were in attendance were skeptical of a Wolverine victory but were excited and ready to go, even before kickoff.

Earle Bruce was an Ohio State assistant at that time. "The fans came into the stadium early," Bruce remembers. "They were loud and rowdy. On my way to the press box, a fan grabbed me and started shaking me and yelling in my face, 'You're going to get yours today, buddy. You're going to get yours today.' Another guy started in on me too. I thought I was going to get into a fight on my way to the press box. I knew right then that Michigan was ready and we might be in trouble."

The Michigan faithful weren't the only ones getting pumped up before the game. When the Wolverines walked out of the tunnel for pre-game warm-ups, they were greeted by the sight of Woody and his players warming up on the Michigan side of the field.

Bo recalls what happened next: "Our players stopped in the tunnel so I went forward to see what the holdup was. Our guys told me that Woody was on our side of the field. Now, I knew this wasn't Woody's first time in Michigan Stadium. He knew exactly what he was doing. He was testing me. He was playing a game of gamesmanship and wanted to get inside my head. I marched out there and said, 'Hey, coach, you're warming up at the wrong end of the field.' With that, Woody grumbled, 'Okay, Bo,' and waved his players down to the other end. Our players saw that and thought I had sent Woody packing. They really got fired up."

One of the things that Michigan coaching staff had stressed all week was containing Rex Kern. They knew that Jim Otis was going to get some yardage, but they felt they couldn't let Kern beat them with his feet. After Tom Campana returned the opening kickoff to the Buckeye 44 yard line, this philosophy was tested.

On the first play from scrimmage, Kern dropped back and then scrambled down the sideline for a 25-yard gain. It was exactly the kind of play the Michigan coaches were worried about. Jim Otis then carried the ball three consecutive times for another first down.

Ohio State was marching down the field and seemed to be picking up right where they had left off in 1968. After a penalty backed the Buckeyes up five yards, Kern hit Otis with a pass to the Michigan 11 yard line to set up fourth-and-two. In subsequent years, Woody would almost assuredly opt for the short field goal in this type of situation early in the game. But his team was moving the ball on Michigan, and no one had stopped his team all year. Hayes decided to go for it.

Otis rammed into the line but was stuffed by Henry Hill, Mike Taylor, and Brian Healey. The fired-up Wolverine defense stormed off the field after the stop to an ovation from the Michigan crowd.

The Ohio State defense answered the stop by forcing a three-and-out on Michigan's first possession, and the Wolverines would have to punt from their goal line.

Larry Zelina fielded the punt at midfield on the run. He split the Michigan defenders and broke a tackle by Garvie Craw at the 27 yard line before being knocked out of bounds by punter Mark Werner at the 15. For the second time in the first few minutes of the game, the Buckeyes were threatening.

The Buckeyes didn't waste the excellent return by Zelina. Kern hit Jan White for a first down at the Michigan 5 yard line. Then, on third-and-goal from the 1, Jim Otis dove into the end zone for his 35th career touchdown. Stan White missed the extra point, but Ohio State was up 6-0. It looked like they were on their way to their 23rd consecutive victory.

Glenn Doughty gave Michigan good field position when he returned the ensuing kickoff to the Wolverine 44 yard line. On second down, Don Moorhead hit Mike Oldham for 8 yards and Garvie Craw got the first down on the following play. Moorhead then passed to Jim Mandich for seven yards, and Craw gained

Tight end Jim Mandich rambles into the Buckeye secondary. Mandich finished with six catches for 78 yards. Photo courtesy of the Bentley Historical Library, University of Michigan.

another first down with a 5-yard run. Two plays later, Moorhead again hit Mandich for a nice gain down to the Ohio State 20.

"We surprised them," recalls center Guy Murdock. "Their defense hadn't been challenged all year, and we were mixing up our passing and running plays well. We had them off balance. And we were knocking them off the ball."

The next play gained another first down on a nice wingback counter inside to John Gabler for 11 yards. On first-and-goal from the 9, Don Moorhead ran an option play down to the 3 yard line. As a true Woody Hayes disciple, Bo then put the offense in a fullhouse backfield and gave the ball to the fullback. Garvie Craw smashed into the end zone, carrying two defenders with him as the crowd went crazy. After Frank Titus kicked the extra point, the score was 7-6 Michigan and the Buckeyes trailed for the first time in the 1969 season.

Being behind for the first time since the Rose Bowl didn't seem to phase the Ohio State offense. Kern passed to Zelina for one first down, then hit Jan White on a tight end drag route across the middle for a big 28-yard gain down to the Michigan 30. After Jim Otis plowed forward for a nine-yard run, Kern got another first down on a quarterback keeper.

The Buckeyes made it look easy as they marched methodically down the field. After a fumbled pitch on an option play brought up third-and-fourteen, the first quarter ended.

On the first play of the second quarter, Kern and White struck again. Kern dumped a short pass over the middle to White who raced toward the sideline. White outran Tom Curtis and a diving Brian Healey to the corner as he scampered into the end zone.

"We felt really good about what we were doing up to that point. But something changed after that. Bo had those guys so well prepared," recalls Kern.

Stan White kicked the extra point, but Michigan was penalized for being offsides. Instead of taking a 13-7 lead, Woody felt confident enough with the half-the-distance penalty that he decided to go for two to make up for the previous miss. Kern rolled out to pass but was chased down by Cecil Pryor and Mike Keller, and sacked.

Michigan's lead had been short-lived as Ohio State went back in front 12-7. Even though they had given up a touchdown, the momentum seemed to swing to the Michigan defense on that play. They wouldn't relinquish it for the rest of the game.

The remaining 14:52 of the first half would be one of the most significant and exciting quarters in Michigan football history. Glenn Doughty had another good return on the ensuing kickoff, and Michigan started their drive on their own 33. Moorhead continued to keep the Ohio State defense off balance by hitting Bill Harris for a first down to the 44 yard line. Moorhead and Gabler runs accounted for ten more yards, and Michigan was again in Buckeye territory.

Mandich then caught another Moorhead pass at the Ohio State 33 and was belted down by Jack Tatum and Tim Anderson. "We had a great game plan," Don Moorhead explains. "We ran off-tackle at them and would then hit Mandich behind their linebackers. It just all worked beautifully that day."

On the next play, Billy Taylor had a magnificent twisting and turning 28-yard run. One of Michigan's favorite plays was 55 Draw and it was executed perfectly. Fullback Garvie Craw chopped down Tatum on the corner and Taylor cut outside. He broke tackles by Provost and Sensibaugh, stopped on a dime to let another defender run past him, and was finally knocked out of bounds by Mark Debevec on the Buckeye 5.

The ecstatic Michigan Stadium crowd went crazy, and they got even louder when Craw pounded in for his second touchdown of the day two plays later. Titus's extra point was good, and Michigan led a shocked Ohio State team 14-12.

The electricity was palpable in the stadium, and the Michigan defense fed off it. They shut down the Buckeye offense in three plays on the following possession and forced a punt.

Mike Sensibaugh boomed a punt that came into Barry Pierson's hands at the Michigan 38. Pierson shot through the first wave of defenders and was off to the races. He set up blocks downfield as he wound his way though Ohio State territory before he was finally brought down at the 3 yard line by Sensibaugh and Bruce Jankowski.

It wasn't Pierson's first long return of the year, but it was the biggest. "We had actually had about five or six long returns like that earlier in the year," Pierson remembers. "Back then, the first wave of defenders didn't come down under control and one move would often help you break free. After I got past them, my teammates did a great job blocking downfield. I just followed them. It couldn't have come at a better time."

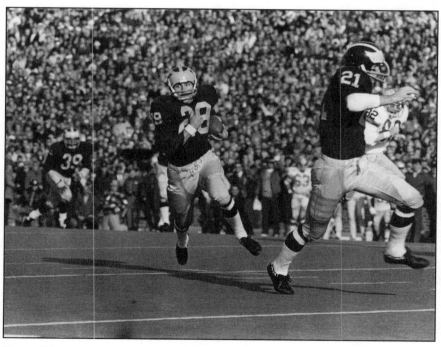

Barry Pierson breaks into the clear on a 60-yard punt return in the second quarter. PHOTO COURTESY OF THE BENTLEY HISTORICAL LIBRARY, UNIVERSITY OF MICHIGAN.

ABC broadcaster Bill Fleming commented on the reaction of the crowd: "Michigan Stadium is in absolute bedlam!"

Two plays later, Moorhead faked to Craw, who was swallowed up by the Ohio State defense, and ran into the end zone. After Titus made his third extra point of the day, Michigan led 21-12.

Jerry Hanlon was Michigan's offensive line coach that day. "You could tell that Ohio State was shocked," said Hanlon. "They hadn't really been tested all year and usually, by this point in the game, they had already knocked out their opponents. But our players were taking it to them."

Even though they were in an incredibly hostile stadium and in the unfamiliar position of being behind, the Buckeyes fought back. After the kickoff, three straight runs by Kern gave Ohio State a first down near midfield. Jim Otis then ripped off a great 25-yard run on a fullback dive play and, just like that, the Buckeyes were at the Michigan 27.

After a short run by Leo Hayden, Rex Kern was flushed from the pocket and sacked back at the 36 by Pete Newell. On third down, Kern's pass fell incomplete and a promising Ohio State drive was stopped.

As the punt team entered the game, a fired-up Michigan defensive unit left the field celebrating to another thunderous ovation. This would be the final trip into Michigan territory for the Buckeyes until the final moments of the game.

The Wolverine offense took over at their 20 yard line and continued to attack the vaunted Ohio State defense. Craw and Moorhead gained a total of eight yards on the first two plays, and then Moorhead ran the option for twelve more and a first down. Michigan continued to mix quick hitting runs by Craw and Taylor with option keepers by Moorhead, and moved the ball down to the Ohio State 34.

"We had to run right at them," Bo recalls. "They were too fast to run away from. A lot of teams would stay away from

Tatum's side, but he'll hunt you down if you do that. We ran and passed right at him."

On third-and-eight from the 34, Moorhead rolled right and fired a pass to a wide open Jim Mandich who raced down to the Buckeye 8 yard line. The Buckeye defense stiffened from there. Michigan faced fourth-and-goal from the 3. Bo Schembechler felt that his team had a firm grasp on the momentum of the game and decided to go for the jugular. Instead of kicking the field goal, Michigan went for it.

Don Moorhead dropped back and rifled a pass into Mandich's hands in the middle of the end zone for a touchdown. The crowd and the Wolverine players all celebrated as no one noticed that there had been a flag on the play. The touchdown was called back and with fourth-and-goal from the 8, Bo decided to kick the field goal. Tim Killian split the uprights, and Michigan had a 24-12 lead.

The teams traded interceptions in the final minute of the first half as Kern threw two and Moorhead threw one. Kern's second interception was a Hail Mary on the final play of the first half. As the Michigan team roared into the locker room, the Ohio State players were in shock but eager to rebound in the second half. No team had scored 24 points on the Buckeyes all season, and Michigan had that at halftime.

George Chaump remembers what went on in the Ohio State locker room. "There was no panicking or heads down. We coached and made adjustments, confident that we would come back and win the game. We were only down by twelve points. We felt that if we could regroup at halftime, we would come out on top."

The scene inside the Michigan locker room was much more animated. "The players were sky high," Bo said. "The coaches were screaming and players were beating on each other. My defensive coordinator, Jim Young, was a very reserved guy. But as he was diagramming plays in front of the team, he began pounding on the blackboard over and over again, saying louder and louder, 'They will NOT score again! They will NOT score again!' After that, there wasn't much for me to say."

Michigan's first drive of the second half started at their own 28 yard line, and they picked up where they had left off before halftime. The Wolverines picked up three first downs and were again in OSU territory as they continued to mix strong runs with Moorhead's passing. The drive was finally stopped by the Ohio State defense at the 30 where Tim Killian attempted a 47-yard field goal. The kick was short of goal line, but the Michigan players downed the ball on the OSU 2 yard line. The Buckeyes moved the ball from the shadow of their own goal posts but were unable to sustain the drive as both teams traded punts on their ensuing possessions.

Ohio State then took over on their own 21 yard line and disaster struck. Henry Hill fought through a double-team block and hit Kern just as he was releasing a pass. The ball sailed high into the air and was picked off by Barry Pierson at the OSU 27. In what would be a recurring theme during the second half, the Ohio State defense rose to the occasion after a turnover gave the ball to Michigan in scoring position. The Wolverines were unable to generate a first down, and Killian missed a 43-yard field goal.

On their next possession, the Buckeyes were victimized by Barry Pierson yet again. Kern lofted a third-down pass deep over the middle, and Pierson snatched it out of the air at the Michigan 28. Pierson returned the interception all the way back to the Ohio State 35 yard line.

"Bo kept telling us all week that he knew what they were going to do," Pierson explains. "He told us that if they put a man in motion or lined up in a certain formation, that this or that would happen. It really hit home to us when that's exactly what they did. We were so confident because Bo had them down cold."

Following the interception, the Michigan offense could only generate one first down, and Killian again missed a field goal attempt.

As the fourth quarter got under way, the Buckeyes again started at their 20 following a missed field goal. After three runs by Jim Otis netted one first down, the Ohio State offense then faced a fourth-and-two from its own 42.

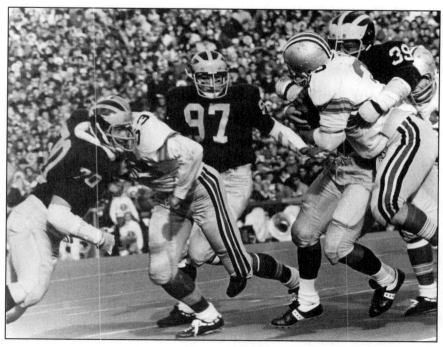

Henry Hill, Marty Huff, and Ed Moore converge on fullback Jim Otis. Otis finished with 144 yards rushing and was the most consistent offensive threat for the Buckeyes. Photo courtesy of the Bentley Historical Library, University of Michigan.

With 13 minutes left in the game, Woody Hayes decided that he needed to go for it instead of punting the ball back to Michigan. From the fullhouse backfield, Kern faked a hand-off to Otis, then ran left. Pete Newell fought off a block, shot into the backfield, and tackled Kern for a loss.

The Michigan defense celebrated wildly as they ran off the field to a thunderous ovation from their fans. The Michigan Stadium crowd was sensing that a huge upset was approaching if Ohio State couldn't do something very quickly.

After the big stop, Michigan took possession at the Ohio State 40 yard line. The Wolverines were able to eat time off the clock by getting two first downs. The second one came on a 7-yard pass from Moorhead to Mike Oldham on a fourth-and-six play. The Buckeye defense eventually stiffened and stuffed Garvie Craw on fourth-and-one from the OSU 10. This kept Ohio State in the game. But now, the clock was definitely becoming a factor.

The Michigan defense again rose up and forced a three-and-out by Ohio State. "Bo had them ready to play," Rex Kern recalls. "It seemed they were in our huddle and knew exactly what we were going to do."

Following a bad bounce on the punt, the Wolverines again started a drive deep in OSU territory. For the second straight time, the Ohio State defense again rose to the occasion and stopped Garvie Craw on a fourth-and-one play to get the ball back for their offense with under seven minutes left in the game.

At this point, Woody decided to make a change at quarterback. Ron Maciejowski was brought in to try to breathe life into an Ohio State offense that was gasping its last breath. If the Buckeyes were going to come back to win the game, it had to be now.

Maciejowski scrambled for one first down. But two plays later, Barry Pierson struck again. The Buckeye backup committed the cardinal sin of throwing late over the middle, and Pierson made him pay. Pierson's third interception gave Michigan the ball at their own 47 yard line.

With only 6:01 remaining, the Wolverines wanted to keep the clock running. Glenn Doughty ripped off runs of 11 and 12 yards, and set UM up in Ohio State territory yet again. For the sixth time in the second half, the Ohio State defense stiffened as Michigan approached scoring range. Once again, Tim Killian missed a field goal.

The Buckeyes took over at the 20 with only 3:12 left. Truly, it was now or never.

On third down, Maciejowski threw a perfect strike downfield to Dick Kuhn who had streaked past the UM defensive backs. Perhaps personifying the day for Ohio State, the pass went right through Kuhn's hands and fell incomplete. On fourth down, Woody called for a fake punt and Mike Sensibaugh hit a wide-open Larry Zelina for a first down to the OSU 38. Maciejowski then hit Dick Kuhn down the middle for another first down at the Michigan 33 yard line. On the next play, Cecil Pryor and Pete Newell continued their harassment of the Ohio State quarterbacks by sacking Maciejowski back at the UM 41. Undeterred, Maciejowski found Ray Gillian for a first down at the Michigan 22.

But the hopes for a miracle rally were squashed on the next play when Thom Darden intercepted the sixth Buckeye pass of the day and returned it to the OSU 33. Michigan tried to run out the remainder of the clock. But Ohio State was able to stop it with timeouts and got the ball back after a punt with 29 seconds to go.

Fittingly, Ohio State's final play was a fumble by Maciejowski that was recovered by Cecil Pryor. It was the seventh and final turnover forced by the Michigan defense.

As the Michigan offense took the field to run out the final few seconds, the Wolverine sideline turned into pandemonium. As Moorhead took a knee to end the game, the crowd counted

As the last seconds tick off the clock, the Michigan sideline explodes in celebration. Photo courtesy of the Bentley Historical Library, University of Michigan.

down the final seconds. When the clock hit zero, the Michigan players hoisted Schembechler on their shoulders and gave him a victory ride to midfield. There, he met his mentor.

Woody shook his hand and said, "Congratulations."

Fans stormed the field and the ecstatic Michigan players were lost in a sea of celebration. ABC broadcaster Bill Fleming said: "There it is! What has to be the upset of the century!" His partner Lee Grosscup added, "I have NEVER seen a team so emotionally up for a game as this Michigan team was today."

Both teams were mobbed as they tried to make it into the tunnel. Players, coaches, trainers, fans, and police officers formed a logjam at the tunnel entrance. Michigan captain Jim Mandich was carried off the field on the shoulders of his teammates with tears streaming down his face. "That game was the signature event of my life," Mandich would later say.

As euphoria reigned in the Michigan locker room, dejection settled in on the Ohio State team. "We were in shock," says Tom Campana. "They were just ready to play. Frankly, they were much more ready than we were."

In what would have to pass for a post-game press conference, Woody Hayes met with reporters outside the locker room for 30 seconds after the game. "All good things must come to an end and that's what happened today. We got outplayed, outcoached, and outpunched," said Hayes. After a few more remarks, Woody made his way through the barrage of reporters and closed the door.

Michigan fullback Garvie Craw summed up his teammates' feelings by proclaiming to the press: "This is the greatest victory in the history of the world!"

Barry Pierson was one of many heroes that day by intercepting three passes, returning a punt for 60 yards, and playing great in run support. "I was just one guy in a group of guys that all did their job. It was special. It's hard to explain, but

I had an electric feeling after that game that literally lasted for two weeks."

Much like Columbus the previous year, the partying in Ann Arbor lasted well into the night.

Gary Moeller recalls just how important the game was to the Michigan program. "It just changed everything. It legitimized what we were doing and changed the course of the program. It also brought back the rivalry. Michigan hadn't had much success against Ohio State in recent years, but this was the turning point. It was going to be a clash of titans from then on."

Bo agrees. "That set the table. There would be no more bad facilities or hanging our clothes on nails. That win ushered in a new era of Michigan football that we are still enjoying today. You can trace it all back to November 22, 1969."

The wild celebration carried into the Wolverine locker room. Garvie Craw, Jim Mandich, and Jack Harping rejoice with their teammates. Photo courtesy of the Bentley Historical Library, University of Michigan.

Ohio State football historian Jack Park called the game the most significant game in Big Ten history. "It was probably Ohio State's most devastating loss ever and probably Michigan's greatest win ever. It changed the course of the conference."

One other thing it did was set up the 1970 game. "Woody didn't wait for the trip home to start preparing for Michigan the next year. He started in the locker room at Michigan Stadium," Tom Campana remembers. "From that moment on, the Michigan game took on a whole new meaning."

A few days after the game, the Michigan team took care of a final piece of unfinished business at its annual football banquet. The game ball from the victory was given to former coach Bump Elliot. "With everything that had happened, it felt really good to be able to give Bump that game ball and I know the players loved it," Bo remembers. "I just have so much respect for that 1969 team. They could have quit on me when I came in. I was so hard on them, but they didn't complain. They did what we asked of them and still loved their former coach Bump Elliot. That was special."

Michigan was headed to the Rose Bowl to face USC. But the morning of the game, Bo Schembechler suffered a heart attack and had to miss the game. His sudden illness took a toll on the Wolverines who lost to the Trojans 10-3. Michigan ended the year ranked #9 while Ohio State would finish ranked #4.

After Woody Hayes left coaching in 1978, a banquet was held for all his former players and staff. Bo was chosen to speak as the representative for Hayes' assistant coaches. As Hayes was speaking, he began to talk about which was his greatest team at Ohio State. After considering it, he chose the 1969 team. He went on to discuss how much talent they had, how good the defense was, and what good chemistry and leadership they possessed. He then paused, look down the dais, and said, "Damn you, Bo! You will NEVER win a bigger game than that one."

Woody was right.

#12 MICHIGAN	**24**
#1 OHIO STATE	**12**

The Game 1969 — Ann Arbor, Michigan

	Michigan	Ohio State
Total Yards	374	377
Rushing Yards	266	222
Passing Yards	108	155
First Downs	21	20
Turnovers	1	7

Key Individual Stats:

JIM MANDICH — 6 catches, 78 yards

BILLY TAYLOR — 23 carries, 84 yards

DON MOORHEAD — 10-20-108 yards / 17 carries, 68 yards, 1TD

JIM OTIS — 22 carries, 144 yards, 1TD

THE GAME 1970

IF THE SEEDS OF THE 1969 GAME WERE SOWN on the grass field of Ohio Stadium in 1968, then the 1970 game was planted on the Tartan Turf of Michigan Stadium in 1969. As the jubilant Michigan players were celebrating their enormous win over Ohio State, the Buckeyes were already looking ahead to 1970. The disappointment and anger over a loss can become a tremendous source of motivation and revenge. The Michigan players understood that in 1969, and the Ohio State players drew the same conclusion a year later. "Remember Ann Arbor" was the rallying cry around Columbus all winter, spring, and summer of 1970 and everyone involved in the Ohio State program remembered all too well.

Despite the bitter loss to Michigan in the 1969 season finale, most were predicting another Ohio State powerhouse in 1970. After winning the National Championship in 1968 and running roughshod over their opposition in 1969, the "Super Sophomores" were now experienced seniors. They were once again loaded with talent on both sides of the ball and hungry for vengeance against "that team up north."

Rex Kern was back for his third season as starting quarterback, after having finished third in Heisman voting in 1969, and would split time with back-up Ron Maciejowski. All-American Jim Otis had graduated; but the backfield remained well stocked with Leo Hayden, John Brockington, and Rick Galbos each getting a good share of carries. Larry Zelina, Bruce Jankowski,

Jan White, and Tom Campana gave either quarterback plenty of talented targets to throw the ball to.

The offensive line was again one of the strengths of the team with All-Conference pick Dave Cheney combining with future All-American John Hicks at the critical tackle spots. Tom DeLeone took over at center while Phil Strickland and Dick Kuhn manned the guard positions.

As in the previous two seasons, the defense was again one of the best in the country. All-American Jim Stillwagon was back at the middle guard position and won both the Lombardi and Outland Trophies. Mark Debevc, Ken Luttner, George Hasenohrl, and Ralph Holloway formed the rest of a very strong defensive line, while Stan White and Doug Adams handled the linebacking chores. The secondary was absolutely loaded. Jack Tatum, Mike Sensibaugh, and Tim Anderson would each be voted onto at least one All-American team in 1970 and Harry Howard would play a great game against Michigan.

Although Ohio State would enter the match-up with Michigan undefeated, they weren't the devastating machine that they had been in 1969. They struggled in wins against Duke, Illinois, and Northwestern and needed a last second field goal to beat Purdue the week prior to the Michigan game. While the defense continued to shut down most opponents, the offense had taken a step back from the previous year.

"After we lost to Michigan in 1969, Woody really handcuffed us on offense," Rex Kern explains. "Because of the number of turnovers and mistakes we had in the Michigan game, Woody would not give us the offensive freedom we had the previous two years. Usually, the more experience you have, the more liberty you would be given in the decision-making process. But the opposite happened to us. It was because of the loss to Michigan in 1969. After that game, Woody reverted back to his pre-1968 mentality. I believe that affected our offense in 1970. I talked to Northwestern coach Alex Agase after the season, and he said that Woody had done the rest of the Big Ten coaches a favor. He said that instead of facing the Cadillac offense that he expected when he played us, he faced one that resembled a Model-T."

After his remarkable rookie season as Michigan head coach, Bo Schembechler put together an even stronger team his second year. The 1970 Wolverines would come into Columbus with a record of 10-0 and a chance to become the first Michigan team to finish undefeated since 1948. The mental and physical toughness that Bo instilled in the program had now had two years to take root.

Don Moorhead was back at quarterback, and his passing and running skills had improved from the year before. The offensive line was one of the best in the country and featured All-American and future NFL Hall of Fame tackle Dan Dierdorf. Reggie McKenzie and Guy Murdock were both All-Big Ten selections while Jack Harping and Tom Coyle rounded out the front wall. This line opened holes for a talent-rich backfield that included tailback Billy Taylor, wingback Glenn Doughty, and fullback Fritz Seyferth. Split end Paul Staroba and tight end Paul Seymour were Moorhead's favorite receiving targets.

Michigan's defense had taken a leap forward from the previous season. They recorded three shutouts and held three other opponents to ten points or less. Mike Keller, Henry Hill, Phil Seymour, Tom Beckman, and Pete Newell were the nucleus of a deep and very quick defensive line. Mike Taylor and Marty Huff were a good pair of linebackers while Frank Gusich, Bruce Elliott, Thom Darden, and Jim Betts formed a very solid secondary.

The Wolverines were tested twice early in the season, against Arizona and Texas A&M, but seemed to be peaking late in the season. In the six games leading up to the Ohio State clash, Michigan had beaten their opponents by an average score of 38-8.

During spring practices, Woody Hayes had a large rug made that was placed right outside the Buckeye dressing room. Each day, the players would have to walk over the rug on their way to the practice field. The message on the rug was simple, yet very powerful. It had the score from the 1969 Michigan-Ohio State game as well as question marks next to the score for the 1970 game. From the second the final gun sounded at Ann Arbor the previous November, Woody and the Ohio State program had been preparing for their chance at revenge in Columbus.

Woody Hayes walks over the rug he had made to remind his players of their goal for 1970. Photo courtesy of the Ohio State University Photo Archives.

This would also be the first time that Ohio State and Michigan would meet in their annual season finale when both teams were undefeated. Due to the Big Ten's no-repeat rule (which would be repealed in 1972), Michigan would be ineligible to go to the Rose Bowl even if they defeated Ohio State. A win would, however, give them an 11-0 record and give them a very good chance at winning the National Championship. On the other hand, even if Ohio State lost the game, their win over Purdue had more or less guaranteed their selection as the conference representative to Pasadena. But all of those things were of secondary importance.

The ultimate goal of both teams would be to win "The Game."

Due to the Buckeyes' close win at Purdue, Michigan had passed them in the AP poll as the Wolverines were ranked #4 while Ohio State came in at #5. Despite being at Columbus, the game was considered to be a toss-up by the odds makers.

Michigan State head coach Duffy Daugherty had faced both teams and wasn't shy about offering his opinion about who he thought would win. "Michigan will beat them," the veteran Spartan coach told reporters at a Tuesday press conference. "Michigan is quicker up front and stronger where Ohio State is strong. Brockington and Hayden will not be able to control the ball on the ground, and Ohio State will be forced to pass."

While not predicting a winner, retired Purdue coach Jack Mollenkopf did get wrapped up in all the hype that surrounded the game. "This will make the Michigan State-Notre Dame game of 1966 look like a tea party."

At that time, it probably was one of the most hyped games ever. The entire Ohio State campus was caught up in the hysteria. Woody even took his players out of their dorm rooms two days before their usual trip to the hotel on Friday night. The student body was getting ready for the game early in the week, and Woody wanted to make sure his players got their rest.

"The excitement around campus the week of the Michigan game was like something I've never experienced before," Rex Kern recalls.

Practice at Ohio State that week wasn't going as well as Woody had hoped. Earle Bruce recalls showing up at the football offices early on Thursday morning. "We walked into the meeting room and found Woody sitting with his head in his hands. We sat around for a few minutes waiting for him to say something. Finally, he just shook his head and said, 'We can't beat them' a few times and put his head back into his hands. He said that instead of getting embarrassed that he would just line up in the fullhouse formation all day and just run the fullback every play to keep the clock running. That way the score wouldn't get too far out of hand."

Bruce continues. "We were shocked. We had worked on our game plan all year, and it was a very good one. Then, all of a sudden, he just decided that we couldn't beat them. We tried to talk to him and tell him we were ready, but he just shook his head and sat there in silence. This went on for literally a few hours. Now, I knew him very well and I knew he liked to play mind games to motivate people. But this wasn't an act. This was despair. Finally, we all got together and decided we had to get him back up."

Bruce remembers what happened next. "We told him that the players couldn't see him like this or they'd start doubting themselves and us. We told him, when the players showed up later, to smash his water pitcher against the wall to get their attention and to fire them up. He wondered if that was a good idea, but we told him that only he could pull it off. So that's what he did. When the players came to the meeting, Woody got in front of them and exploded into a rage and smashed the pitcher against the wall. That really got their attention and things really picked up after that."

Rex Kern also remembers Woody's unique way of motivating his team that week. "We were doing a walk through where you move down the field talking about different plays and situations," Kern explains. "When we got to midfield, Woody stopped to stress an important point and, out of the corner of his eye, he noticed two players who were still back at the goal line talking to each other. Well, that did it. He took his play cards he was using and began tearing them up and threw them across the field. He started screaming at the top of his lungs. 'Don't you guys know who we're playing? Don't you know it's Michigan? It's Michigan! It's Michigan!'

"He tore off his watch, threw it down, and stomped on it. He started crying real tears and fell down on the ground, pounding his fists on the ground. By this time, the two players who hadn't been paying attention were running, at full sprint, toward midfield. Earle Bruce came over to help Woody up. As he was getting Woody to his feet, Woody just kept whimpering, 'They won't play for me, Earle. They just won't play for me.' Earle kept saying, 'Sure they will, coach. Sure, they'll play for you.' As Woody was putting himself back together, some of our younger guys like John Hicks and Tom DeLeone, who were very emotional guys, were almost beside themselves and kept telling me, 'C'mon, Rex. Get us moving. Get us going.' It was a very effective motivational tactic. That practice really sharpened us up after that. It was vintage Woody."

After all the brutal practices and all the media hype, Saturday finally arrived with beautiful, sunny skies and mild temperatures. The entire city of Columbus was exploding with excitement. The Ohio Stadium crowd was as mentally ready for the game as the two teams were. This was what everyone had been waiting an entire year for, and they were eager to get started.

John Hicks remembers the crowd getting to the game very early. "We came out for warm-ups about an hour and a half before kickoff, and the stadium was almost full already. It was incredible."

The players were sky high with emotion, and it showed on the opening kickoff. Michigan's Lance Scheffler caught the kick at the 12 yard line and headed up field. He was belted by Rich Ferko at the 22 and fumbled. Ohio State's Harry Howard dove on the ball at the 25 yard line and, just like that, the Buckeyes were in business.

"That was a huge play for them," Michigan assistant Jerry Hanlon remembers. "The crowd was already fired up and, all of a sudden, they've got the ball. That's a tough way to start out on the road."

The Buckeye offense went right for the jugular. On second down, Kern fired a pass to Bruce Jankowski on a hook pattern at the 14. Jankowski caught the ball and was hit in the legs before regaining his balance and running into the corner of the end zone for a touchdown. But the official was right on top of the play and ruled that Jankowski's knee hit the ground at the 14. Ohio State had a first down deep in Michigan territory but felt that they had been robbed of a touchdown. Michigan's defense tightened up, and Fred Schram came in to kick a 28-yard field goal to give Ohio State a 3-0 lead early in the first quarter.

Both offenses managed to get a couple first downs on their next few possessions, but neither team could mount much of a threat against the opposing defense. Michigan pinned the Buckeyes back at their own 1 yard line following a punt on one of these possessions and hoped to get the ball back in excellent field position. But Ohio State pounded fullback John Brockington up the middle to get one first down and sent Leo Hayden off tackle on sprint-draws very effectively. This drive eventually stalled, but it did get the Buckeyes out of awful field position.

Near the end of the first quarter, Kern threw a pass over the middle that was intercepted by safety Jim Betts at the OSU 43. Betts returned the pick to the 18 yard line. With their offense struggling to open holes or move the ball against the aggressive Buckeye defense, this was just the break Michigan needed. But the Wolverines couldn't get near the goal line and after a third down pass fell incomplete in the end zone, Dana Coin kicked a 31-yard field goal early in the second quarter to tie the game at 3-3.

The defenses continued to control play through most of the second quarter as Ohio State had success running the ball but couldn't sustain drives while Michigan was running into a brick wall. Moorhead was able to complete a few passes, but the Wolverine running game was being stuffed by the Buckeye defense. Michigan had entered the game averaging 274 yards rushing, but the ferocious Ohio State defenders were cutting off any running lanes and stopping the talented Wolverine running backs in their tracks.

Billy Taylor found little, very little, running room as the powerful Michigan ground game was completely shut down by the Buckeye defense.

PHOTO COURTESY OF BROCKWAY SPORTS PHOTOS.

The game's next big play was a needless penalty. Paul Staroba nailed a booming 73-yard punt with the wind that backed Ohio State up to their 18 yard line. But a face-mask penalty, while the ball was in the air, nullified the kick and Staroba was forced to punt from his end zone. His next kick wasn't nearly as good, and the Buckeyes took over at the UM 47. The unnecessary face-mask penalty had given Ohio State 35 yards of field position.

The Buckeye offense didn't squander the opportunity. They moved down the field on the legs of Brockington and Hayden. One play that was very effective was the sprint-draw to Leo Hayden.

"We had watched a ton of film of Michigan all year," right tackle Dave Cheney explains. "One of the things they were predictable about was the way they slanted toward the short side of the field. On that sprint-draw, we would pull the backside guard and Kern would give the ball to Hayden after they both gave the look of a pass play. It was very effective, and we gained a lot of yards off of that."

At the Michigan 29 yard line, Ohio State faced a fourth-and-three situation. It was too far away for a good chance at a field goal and too close to punt, so the Buckeyes went for it. Kern ran a perfect option play for four yards to give Ohio State a crucial first down. After two running plays didn't gain anything, the Buckeyes were again faced with a critical play on third-and-ten at the UM 25.

"I called an audible at the line for Gold 98," Kern remembers. "We called it 'Gold' because Woody said every time we ran that play, it was good as gold."

Gold 98 was a post pattern to Bruce Jankowski. Kern dropped back and faced heavy pressure from a blitz by linebacker Marty Huff. Just before he was leveled, Kern threw the ball to where he knew Jankowski would be.

"I didn't see Bruce catch the ball," Kern recalls. "After I was hit, I just laid there and listened for the crowd's reaction. When I heard them roar, I knew we hit it. I had a Michigan player on top of me and I just kissed the top of that helmet."

Jankowski had beaten Bruce Elliott inside by just a few inches, but it was a perfectly executed play. Safety Jim Betts couldn't get over in time as Jankowski caught the ball at the 5 yard line and raced into the end zone without breaking stride. After Schram's extra point, the score was 10-3 with only 1:18 left in the half.

Michigan tried to get into scoring territory when they got the ball back. But disaster struck. Moorhead passed to Billy Taylor in the flat at the UM 36. Taylor caught the ball and ran to the 45, where he was hit hard by Jack Tatum and Harry Howard, and fumbled. Linebacker Stan White fell on the loose football at the Michigan 46 yard line. With 39 seconds left in the second quarter, the Buckeyes were threatening again.

On first down, Kern rolled right and hit wingback Tom Campana, who was playing in place of the injured Larry Zelina, for nineteen yards to the Michigan 27. After a Hayden run gained four more yards, a timeout was called to stop the clock. A few plays later, there was some confusion about whether to send in the field goal unit or to try to get a few more yards. It ended up costing Ohio State. After a short pass to Hayden kept the clock running, the Buckeyes desperately tried to get another play off to stop it as time ran out. The half ended with Ohio State leading 10-3.

The Ohio State game plan had worked very well in the first half.

"We knew what we wanted to do and it was working," Dave Cheney recalls. "We were excited at halftime, but we knew we each had a job to do. Our defense was just playing incredibly. That was the difference in the game."

The Ohio State defense was controlling the line of scrimmage. Michigan had a great offensive line, but the Buckeyes were doing a tremendous job of shutting them down.

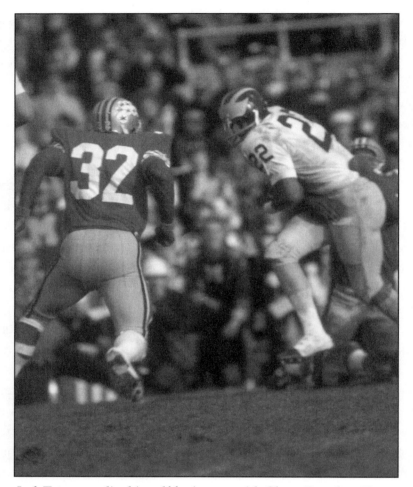

Jack Tatum readies himself for impact with Glenn Doughty. Tatum led a hard-hitting defense that controlled the game. PHOTO COURTESY OF BROCKWAY SPORTS PHOTOS.

The Michigan offense was frustrated but still felt like the game was still up for grabs, which it was.

"We just weren't playing well," Reggie McKenzie explains. "A lot of that was the Ohio State defense, but we just weren't executing well."

Quarterback Don Moorhead agrees. "We just couldn't move the ball on the ground. I really felt like we were going to have to pass more if we were going to win. They were stuffing our running game and, back then, that was our strength. We probably should have opened things up a little more."

The second half started promisingly for Michigan as they forced a three-and-out by the Ohio State offense and got the ball back at midfield. After a penalty, Michigan faced a third-and-eight from the OSU 48. Moorhead converted the first down by hitting Paul Staroba with a 12-yard pass to the Ohio State 36 yard line. Moorhead and Staroba connected again for 9 yards on a third-and-ten play to set up fourth-and-inches from OSU 26. Fullback Fritz Seyferth got the call and plowed ahead for two yards and the first down.

On what would be their best drive of the day, the Michigan offense converted another third down on a Seyferth plunge to give the Wolverines a first down at the OSU 13. Two plays later, Moorhead rolled left and lofted a pass to Staroba, who had beaten Harry Howard to the back corner of the end zone. Staroba's touchdown would have tied the game, but Tim Anderson knifed in to block Dana Coin's extra point attempt and the Buckeyes held on to the lead at 10-9.

Michigan kept the pressure on by again forcing a three-and-out by Ohio State on the next two possessions. Each time the Wolverines would get the ball at midfield, and each time the Buckeye defense wouldn't budge.

"That was story of the game that day," Bo explains. "They did a great job of shutting down our running game. We didn't do a good job of knocking them off the line. But you have to give the credit to Ohio State."

After Jim Stillwagon sacked Moorhead for a 7-yard loss on a third-and-thirteen play, Michigan was forced to punt and the Buckeyes took over at the OSU 27. As the third quarter came to a close, Ohio State gained their initial first down of the second half on a draw play by Leo Hayden. The Ohio State ground game was now back on track with Hayden, Rick Galbos, and John Brockington finding running room behind great blocking by the offensive line.

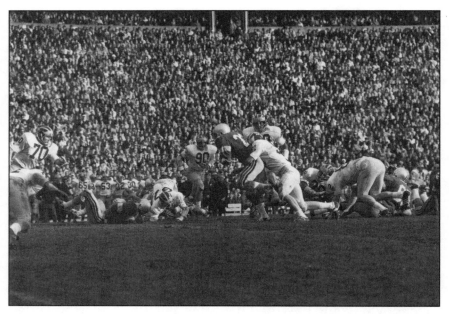

Tailback Leo Hayden led all rushers with 118 yards and hurt Michigan repeatedly on the sprint-draw play. PHOTO COURTESY OF THE OHIO STATE UNIVERSITY PHOTO ARCHIVES.

Kern hit tight end Jan White for a 16-yard completion down to the UM 11. But there, the Michigan defense stiffened. Fred Schram kicked his second field goal of the day and with 10:49 left in the game, the Buckeyes led 13-9.

The field goal gave Ohio State a little breathing room. The drive was also important because it flipped field position. After playing the entire third quarter in Ohio State territory, Michigan would have to start their next drive on their own end of the field.

Michigan was running out of time. Now, they would need a touchdown to win instead of a field goal. With their running game crushed and with the clock becoming a factor, they would have to rely on the pass. Being behind in a very hostile stadium put even more pressure on the offense. And they cracked.

After Jim Stillwagon and Shad Williams combined to sack Moorhead on second down, the Wolverines faced third-and-thirteen. Moorhead rolled to his left, faked a draw handoff to Billy Taylor, and fired a pass over the middle towards Paul Seymour. He didn't see linebacker Stan White. White picked off the pass at the 25 and returned to the Michigan 9 yard line as the Ohio Stadium crowd exploded. With 9:30 left in the game, the Buckeye defense had again come up with a big play.

Sensing that another Ohio State score would seal the win, the Michigan defense dug in to try to hold.

"If we could hold them to a field goal, we'd still be within a touchdown," safety Thom Darden explains. "We knew that if they put it in the end zone, we would really be in trouble so we did everything we could to keep them out."

After runs by Brockington and Kern gained five yards, the Buckeyes were looking at third-and-goal from the Michigan 4 yard line. The Buckeyes lined up in the fullhouse backfield. Michigan crowded the line scrimmage with ten defenders. At the snap, Kern spun around, faked a handoff to fullback John Brockington, and ran down the line. Right tackle John Hicks made a great block to seal the corner, and Kern forced Darden to commit to him before pitching out to Hayden. Hayden took the pitch at the 7 and ran into the end zone untouched.

Toilet paper and confetti rained down onto the celebrating Buckeye players as the crowd erupted. Schram made the extra point and, with 8:14 left, Ohio State held a commanding 20-9 lead.

Things then went from bad to worse for Michigan. Preston Henry and Bo Rather bobbled the ensuing kickoff in the end zone, and Rather was tackled at the 2 yard line. The fired-up Ohio State defense continued to control the tempo of the game as

Michigan was unable to gain a first down. The Wolverines were forced to punt. But they got a break when the officials ruled that Tim Anderson touched the ball as he was watching the punt roll dead. Reggie McKenzie fell on the ball at midfield and Michigan was awarded possession. (Replays would show that Anderson did not touch the ball, although he did get very close to it.)

This break seemed to breathe some life into the Michigan offense as Moorhead hit Taylor for 12 yards on one play and Staroba for 8 on the next. Preston Henry then gained a first down on a 4-yard run to the OSU 26. Michigan was still alive.

After two incompletions and a 3-yard draw play to Taylor, the Wolverines faced fourth-and-seven at the OSU 23. If they were to have any hope of a comeback, they needed to convert on this play. Moorhead dropped back to pass and had great protection. He fired a perfect pass to a wide-open Glenn Doughty at the 12 yard line, but the ball hit Doughty square in the chest and fell incomplete.

Taking over at their own 23 with 4:58 remaining, the Buckeyes wanted to run out what was left of the clock. Hayden and Brockington kept the clock moving by getting first downs on two third-down plays as Ohio State moved towards midfield. Rick Galbos then electrified the crowd by ripping off a 32-yard run up the middle to the Michigan 21 yard line. Galbos took the handoff, darted through the hole, ran over a tackler at the 45, and raced down the sideline.

That sealed it.

Galbos, Brockington, and Kern each carried one more time before the final gun sounded. The crowd poured out onto the field as the Ohio State players celebrated with them.

"That was special," Dave Cheney remembers. "After that 1969 loss to Michigan, we had been pointing to this for an entire year. It was redemption."

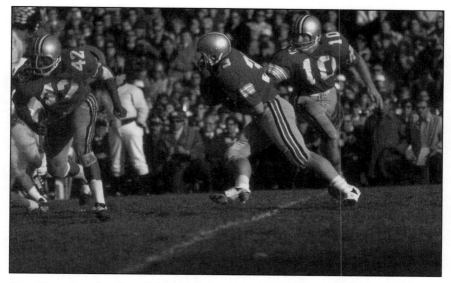

Rex Kern hands off to Rick Galbos as John Brockington blocks late in the fourth quarter. PHOTO COURTESY OF BROCKWAY SPORTS PHOTOS.

The celebration lasted well into the night around Columbus. Students even carried one of the goal posts downtown to the Statehouse.

"It's hard to describe how much that win meant to us and to Woody," Rex Kern explains. "That loss at Ann Arbor was so bitter that it made the win in 1970 that much sweeter."

Ohio State's locker room was a sea of celebration as Ohio Governor James Rhodes addressed the team, and President Richard Nixon called to congratulate his close friend Woody Hayes.

Woody beamed as he conducted his post-game press conference. "I've got to feel that this was our greatest victory," he told the gathered reporters. Always the military historian when asked where he picked up the sprint-draw play that was so effective, Woody drew upon examples from history. "Michigan refined it. I saw it in their highlight reels from last year. I truly relish turning an opponent's play against him. It's a funny thing.

The Japanese got their plan for attacking Pearl Harbor from our own Fleet Problem Number 14 of 1934. The Germans got the tank from the British."

The win is still considered one of the greatest in Ohio State history. It was also one of the best defensive performances the Buckeyes have ever produced. Michigan, who had been averaging 274 yards rushing per game, only gained 37 yards on the ground against the Ohio State defense. That was the difference in the game.

Ohio State would climb to #2 in the polls and would play for the National Championship in Pasadena after the defeat of top-ranked Texas in the Cotton Bowl. The Buckeyes held a 17-13 lead early in the final quarter and had the ball at the Stanford 19 yard line. But John Brockington was stopped on a fourth-and-inches play and Heisman winner Jim Plunkett led his team to two late touchdowns to upset Ohio State 27-17.

Regardless of the outcome of the Rose Bowl, the 1969 and 1970 Michigan-Ohio State games set the tone for the Ten Year War and also raised the bar for every edition of "The Game" to follow. The emotion and excitement that these games generated would be played out, again and again, over the next eight seasons.

#5 OHIO STATE	20
#4 MICHIGAN	9

The Game 1970 — Columbus, Ohio

	Ohio State	Michigan
Total Yards	329	155
Rushing Yards	242	37
Passing Yards	87	118
First Downs	18	10
Turnovers	2	3

Key Individual Stats:

LEO HAYDEN — 26 carries, 118 yards, 1TD

JOHN BROCKINGTON — 27 carries, 77 yards

REX KERN — 8-12-87 yards-1TD

THE GAME 1971

" T HOSE GAMES WERE JUST SO EMOTIONAL. You can't quantify that. Forget all about favorites or underdogs or who has the better record. Sheer emotion can be the great equalizer." This statement by Michigan assistant and future head coach Gary Moeller is probably the best description of the 1971 game.

Emotion allowed a young team that had been decimated by injuries to almost win a game they had no business keeping close, and emotion caused a legendary coach to have a legendary meltdown. One thing is certain: anyone who witnessed the game in Michigan Stadium that day has never forgotten it.

Bo Schembechler had worked wonders in Ann Arbor since taking over the program in 1969. Michigan was now regarded as one of the nation's premier programs, and the success that the 1971 team enjoyed only added to that perception. The Wolverines rolled over their opposition en route to a 10-0 record and #3 ranking heading into the Ohio State game. Only Purdue had stayed within a touchdown of Michigan, and many of the games were essentially over at halftime.

The Wolverines led the nation in scoring defense by allowing only 6.3 points per game and were first in rushing defense and third in total defense. Butch Carpenter, Fred Grambau, Greg Ellis, Tom Beckman, Mike Keller, Tom Kee, and

All-American Mike Taylor made up one of the better front sevens in the country. The secondary of Randy Logan, Frank Gusich, Bruce Elliott, and All-American Thom Darden was also very strong as Michigan recorded three shutouts and held five other teams to one touchdown or less.

Not to be outdone, the Wolverine offense compiled an impressive resume as well. One of the reasons the Michigan defense gave up so few points was that the Michigan offense often held the ball for long periods of time. The offensive line of Jim Brandstatter, Tom Coyle, Jim Coode, Guy Murdock, and All-American Reggie McKenzie paved the way for Michigan to lead the Big Ten in rushing, scoring, and total offense. The ferocious running game featured All-American Billy Taylor, fullbacks Fritz Seyferth and Ed Shuttlesworth, and wingback Glenn Doughty. Senior Tom Slade was a very good running quarterback who wasn't called on to pass very often.

Woody Hayes faced perhaps the most challenging rebuilding project of his career in 1971. Gone were the "Super Sophomores" who had compiled a 27-2 record and won three Big Ten titles in the previous three years. If losing 17 starters to graduation or the NFL wasn't bad enough, the Buckeyes were also hit with an epidemic of injuries that was mind-boggling. By the time the Michigan game arrived, not a single offensive starter from 1970 was on the field.

This was the first year of artificial turf in Ohio Stadium and some blamed it for the rash of injuries. "It tore up people's knees that first year," recalls Van DeCree. Tom Campana remembers Woody taking precautions when they practiced on the new artificial turf. "Woody would water it down before we practiced to keep the traction from being so stiff." Some players started jokingly referring to the artificial practice field as Lake Hayes.

Senior Don Lamka and sophomore Greg Hare shared the quarterback duties, and both of them would be injured at one time or another during the year. The offensive line was anchored by All-American center Tom DeLeone, but he tore up his knee the week before the Michigan game and would have to undergo surgery. Future star John Hicks was slated to start at one tackle spot, but an injury during summer camp caused him to miss the entire season. The line was patched together week to week with whatever available players avoided the ever-increasing disabled list.

Merve Teague, Tom Nixon, Milan Vecanski, Charlie Beecroft, Charles Bonica, Bill Conley, Rick Simon, and Jim Kregel all saw playing time up front as line coach Earle Bruce scrambled to build a solid unit. "We were just crippled with injuries on the line and everywhere else, for that matter. You'd try to find the right combinations. But when you did, someone would get hurt. Then you'd be right back in the same spot the next week."

Rick Galbos led the team in rushing, despite being banged up, and combined with Randy Keith to give Ohio State a good pair of fullbacks. Elmer Lippert and Morris Bradshaw handled the tailback duties while Dick Wakefield, Fred Pagac, Tom Battista, John Smurda, and Jimmie Harris were the tight ends and wideouts.

The Buckeye defense was also injury-riddled and changing week to week. Ken Luttner, Shad Williams, Rich Cappell, Tom Marendt, Mike Scannell, George Hasenohrl, and Dan Cutillo rotated on the defensive line, though Williams was lost to injury in midseason and Luttner often played hurt. The linebacking corps was solid as senior Stan White was the leader of the defense, and sophomores Vic Koegel and Randy Gradishar really matured as the season progressed. The secondary consisted of Tom Campana, Lou Mathis, Rick Seifert, Jeff Davis, Harry Howard, and Bob Kelly, though several of these players missed time due to injuries as some point during the season.

Ohio State lost a close game early in the season to a Colorado team that would finish the year ranked #3. The Buckeyes then rebounded to win five straight before losing consecutive games to Michigan State and Northwestern, the two weeks before the Michigan contest. With a record of 6-3, no one expected the young, injury-depleted Buckeyes to be able to stay with the powerful, undefeated, Big Ten champion Wolverines. The odds makers had tabbed Michigan as an almost two-touchdown favorite.

As usual, practices for both teams were brutal during the week of the game as each player wanted to be at their peak for "The Game." Woody had to back off the hitting a little on Wednesday because the Tuesday practice had been so tense and physical that he knew his team could ill afford any further injuries. Bo felt his team had a good week of practice as well. "We prepared as hard for them as we always did. We didn't take them lightly, that's for sure."

Early Saturday morning, there was a strange development that perfectly summed up Ohio State's season. Tom Marendt, starting defensive end, had an appendicitis attack and would miss the game. The defensive depth went from desperately thin to depleted.

Another record crowd jammed into Michigan Stadium under skies that would change from snow to rain and then to sun.

The Wolverines received the ball to start the game but were forced to punt after three plays. Tom Slade, the Wolverine quarterback, injured his hip on a draw play on third down and Larry Cipa took his place. Barry Dotzauer's kick came down at the OSU 23 into the hands of Tom Campana and the senior began having the game of his life. Campana ran through an arm tackle at the 33, cut outside, juked another defender at the 45, and took off down the sideline. Billy Taylor had an angle and enough speed to trip up Campana at the Michigan 28 yard line, and the Buckeyes had the game's first big play.

Ohio State used runs by Rick Galbos, Elmer Lippert, and Randy Keith to get one first down but a fumbled handoff from Greg Hare to Keith was recovered by Michigan's Greg Ellis at the 17 yard line. It was a costly turnover as the Buckeye offense wouldn't get this close to the Michigan goal line for the remainder of the game.

The Wolverines banged out a few first downs behind the runs of Taylor and Shuttlesworth before a delay-of-game penalty helped kill the drive. Ohio State was forced to punt on their next possession, and when Michigan got the ball back, they moved the ball into Buckeye territory. But on fourth and inches at the OSU 23, George Hasenohrl, Stan White, and Randy Gradishar stuffed Shuttlesworth, and Ohio State took over.

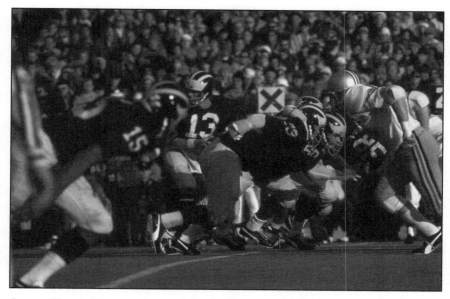

Larry Cipa took over at quarterback after Tom Slade's injury. PHOTO COURTESY OF BROCKWAY SPORTS PHOTOS.

As the first quarter came to a close, the Buckeyes managed to move the ball with runs by Lippert and Galbos and a 16-yard pass completion from Hare to Dick Wakefield. A pass interference call on Mike Keller gave the Buckeyes another first down, but the Michigan defense eventually stiffened and forced a punt. Three plays later, Ohio State was again in Michigan territory after Gradishar forced a Billy Taylor fumble that was recovered by Rick Seifert at the Wolverine 28 yard line. This wasn't converted into points either as Fred Schram was wide left on a 38-yard field goal a few plays later.

Tom Slade came back into the game at quarterback for Michigan, and the Wolverines put together a very good drive. Mixing sweeps and option plays to the outside by Doughty and Taylor with tough, inside running plays by Shuttlesworth and Taylor, Michigan moved deep into Buckeye territory.

"We were running on them pretty well," Shuttlesworth recalls. "We figured we would wear them down as the game went on. But they played very physical defense and were really getting after it." The Ohio State defense finally stopped the drive at the OSU 15, and Dana coin-kicked a 32-yard field goal to give Michigan a 3-0 lead with 5:19 left in the second quarter.

The Wolverines threatened to score again before the half when Thom Darden intercepted a Hare to Tom Battista pass at the OSU 49 and returned it to the 38. After a 5-yard penalty, Tom Slade dropped back and fired a perfect pass to Bo Rather on a post pattern to the 19 yard line. Two Glenn Doughty runs gave Michigan a first-and-goal at the OSU 8, but Billy Taylor fumbled a pitch from Slade and Harry Howard recovered for Ohio State at the 11.

Neither team could do anything on their next possession, and the first half ended with Michigan leading 3-0.

"We had controlled their offense very well in the first half," Thom Darden remembers. "It was frustrating to only be up by a field goal. We stopped them twice deep in our territory after a punt return and a fumble, so we felt confident that we could shut them down." Michigan's running game was gaining yards, but two Billy Taylor fumbles and the inspired Ohio State defense always seemed to stop promising drives. The Wolverine backs were sharing the load as Taylor had 63 yards at the half while both Doughty and Shuttlesworth had 57.

Randy Gradishar recalls what the Buckeyes were thinking at halftime. "We were giving everything we had, and it showed. If you can hold that offense to only three points in a half, you're doing something right. We knew we had a great chance to win the game."

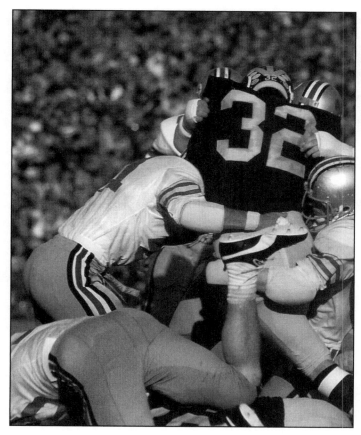

Fullback Fritz Seyferth runs into a determined Ohio State defense that kept the Buckeyes in the game.

PHOTO COURTESY OF BROCKWAY SPORTS PHOTOS.

Ohio State received the ball to start the second half, and Don Lamka came in at quarterback to replace Greg Hare. The Buckeyes gained one first down on their opening drive of the third quarter before being forced to punt. Larry Cipa again relieved Slade at quarterback and marched Michigan past midfield before the drive stalled at the OSU 46.

The sun came out from behind the clouds midway through the third quarter as the weather continued to go back and forth as the game wore on.

Neither team could do anything on their ensuing possessions as the defenses continued to dominate the game. "We had trouble moving the ball," Elmer Lippert recalls. "Our line was patched together from all the injuries and I think with our defense playing the way it was, Woody wanted to play it safe. There was definitely a lot of hard hitting going on." Fullback Rick Galbos agrees, "Our defense was keeping us in the game at that point. We weren't moving the ball very well. But some of that was due to the Michigan defense."

The teams traded punts, and Tom Campana again made his presence felt on a return as he fielded a Dotzauer punt on the OSU 11 and took off up the middle of the field. He was finally knocked out of bounds at the Michigan 39 yard line, but a clipping penalty nullified the excellent return. The Buckeyes would have to start the drive from their 10 yard line so, in effect, the penalty cost them 51 yards that their struggling offense desperately needed.

Ohio State again couldn't move, and neither could Michigan on the following possession as Barry Dotzauer would again kick to Tom Campana.

Campana caught the ball at the OSU 15, split the first wave of defenders, and sprinted up the middle. He eluded two diving tacklers at the 35 yard line and broke into the clear with only Dotzauer to beat. Campana was running at full speed and Dotzauer didn't have much of a chance as Campana gave him a slight head fake and ran past him. As Campana ran into the end zone to give Ohio State the lead, he was mobbed by his teammates. The Buckeyes called a timeout after the touchdown and were penalized for illegal procedure on the first extra point. But Fred Schram nailed his second attempt and, unbelievably, Ohio State had the lead at 7-3 with 2:07 left in the third quarter.

"My teammates did a great job of blocking for me," Campana recalls. "I just tried to follow their blocks and make a few cuts along the way. Once I hit the middle of the field, everything opened up and I just had to make the punter miss."

Both teams punted on their next few possessions as the clock started to become a factor for Michigan. The Wolverines got the ball back at their 28 yard line with only 7:08 remaining in the game and the knowledge that they wouldn't have many more opportunities. The Ohio State defense knew this as well and, despite being tired from spending most of the day on the field, dug in hoping one last stop would allow them claim to the upset.

Michigan almost took the lead on a long pass to Paul Seymour, who had gotten behind the Ohio State secondary, but Cipa overthrew him by a few feet. Billy Taylor then gained a crucial first down on a third-and-seven play by getting 8 yards on a draw play. After two runs set up another third down, Cipa hit Bo Rather for 15 yards to the OSU 40. The play was the 54-55 Draw/Pass where the action looks like a draw but the quarterback rolls out to throw. It was executed perfectly and Michigan now had a first down in Buckeye territory with less than five minutes left.

As the clock continued to roll, Michigan gained a total of 9 yards on three straight runs to set up a fourth-and-one at the Ohio State 24 yard line with only 2:45 remaining. If the Buckeye defense could manage to hold, they could run out the clock and leave Michigan Stadium with a huge upset win.

The Wolverines lined up in a power-I to the right and Fritz Seyferth smashed ahead for 3 yards on a fullback dive for the key first down. On the next play, Cipa ran the option to the right and pitched the ball to Billy Taylor on the outside. Cipa continued down the line to chop down defensive end Rich Cappell while Seyferth made a great block on Tom Campana as Taylor used his speed to go down the sideline into the end zone.

Following the blocks of Larry Cipa and Fritz Seyferth, Billy Taylor breaks to the outside for a 21-yard touchdown run that gave Michigan a 10-7 lead.
PHOTO COURTESY OF THE BENTLEY HISTORICAL LIBRARY, UNIVERSITY OF MICHIGAN.

"Ohio State had been playing ferocious defense all day," Bo recalls. "But on that touchdown run, we ran the speed option. The defense can penetrate up the middle all they want on that play but if you seal the outside, you've got it. Cipa and Seyferth made great blocks on the corner, and Taylor just turned on the jets." As the crowd went crazy, Dana Coin nailed the extra point.

With only 2:07 left, Ohio State would get the ball back. The offense had struggled all day but felt confident as they took the field. "We thought we could do it," Elmer Lippert remembers. "You always believe in yourself and your teammates."

Due to his explosive punt returns, Tom Campana replaced Morris Bradshaw on the kickoff return team so Coin opted to squib the kickoff. Ohio State would begin their drive at the 30 yard line. On first down, the Buckeyes would have their most productive play of the game.

Don Lamka dropped back, was pressured by Mike Keller, and rolled to his right. Dick Wakefield was blocking from the tight end position, but released when he saw Lamka start to scramble. Lamka lofted a pass to Wakefield, who had nothing but open field in front of him, and he rambled down the sideline for 25 yards to the Michigan 45 yard line. Just like that, Ohio State was threatening to get into field goal position with under two minutes left.

After a pass to Bradshaw was incomplete, Ellis, Beckman, and Grambau sacked Lamka on the OSU 49. Ohio State called their final timeout to stop the clock. Now facing third and sixteen, the Buckeyes needed yards. They had two downs to get it in. Lamka dropped back in the pocket and fired a pass towards Wakefield on a crossing pattern. As the ball got to Wakefield, Michigan wolfman Thom Darden jumped over his back to make a leaping interception at the UM 32. As the Wolverine defensive players and the crowd celebrated the turnover, the Ohio State players and bench were screaming for a pass interference penalty to be called. They felt that Darden had gone over Wakefield's back and interfered with him.

Thom Darden still remembers his most famous interception. "I went over the top of Wakefield. I was just trying to knock the ball away but when I came down, the ball was in my hands. I'm glad it happened in Ann Arbor because in Columbus it might have been called interference." Rick Galbos recalls seeing the play. "He came over Wakefield's back. If that's not interference, I don't know what is."

Thom Darden goes over the top of Dick Wakefield for his controversial interception. Note Woody Hayes in background with hands on hips. PHOTO COURTESY OF THE BENTLEY HISTORICAL LIBRARY, UNIVERSITY OF MICHIGAN.

It was at this point that the real fireworks started.

As the ball was being placed down for Michigan's possession, Woody Hayes stormed onto the field. "I had been in the backfield during the play so I didn't see the interception," referee Jerry Markbreit recalls. "I saw one of my deep officials signal that it was Michigan's ball so I knew there had to be a turnover. As I was signaling for play to resume, I look up and see Woody Hayes coming straight towards me. He was 50 yards onto the field, which is obviously a penalty, so I throw a flag. As I was making the call for unsportsmanlike conduct, he was all over me. His face was literally right on my shoulder, and he was calling me every name in the book. He said that as the head of the officiating crew, I needed to overturn the interception. But I didn't even see it. He stayed on me for about five minutes and followed me around the field, yelling in my ear the entire time."

As the fans in the stadium watched in amazement and amusement, Woody continued his verbal assault. After a few minutes, a security guard from the Michigan bench offered to remove Woody from the playing field. But Markbreit waved him off. Finally, Ohio State assistant coach George Chaump and a few Buckeye players managed to drag Hayes back to the Ohio State sideline.

"I've always felt a little regret about the whole incident," Chaump recalls. "After the interception, I told Woody to call a timeout or something because I thought if we could stop play, the officials would realize how flagrant the interference had been and would throw the flag. Of course, I had no idea that he would end up doing what he did."

After Woody was taken to the sideline, the Michigan offense took the field to run out the remaining 1:25 left in the game. But Woody wasn't finished yet.

Larry Cipa twice took the snap and fell down to keep the clock running. But on the second play, Randy Gradishar was penalized and ejected from the game for unnecessary roughness.

"When you eject a player from the game, you have to escort him to the sidelines and explain to his coach why he is being ejected," Markbreit explains. "As I was walking Gradishar back to the sideline, I saw Woody attacking the first down markers. I told Randy he would have to go over there by himself because I wasn't going near Woody at that point."

As Jerry Markbreit marks off a penalty for unsportsmanlike conduct, Woody Hayes was right on his heels and in his ear. Photo courtesy of UPI.

Hayes grabbed the first down marker and broke it over his knee. He then tore the top off the red sideline down marker and tossed it onto the field. George Chaump eventually pulled Woody away from the chain crew and Michigan ran out the remainder of the clock for a 10-7, hard-fought, and controversial victory.

As the fans stormed the field to celebrate, many were still in disbelief about what they had seen the final few moments of the game. "Woody Hayes was a very emotional guy," Jerry Hanlon recalls. "That was an instance where he allowed his emotions to overrule his common sense."

New Big Ten Commissioner Wayne Duke was in attendance that day. It was the first game he attended in person as the new commissioner. (Interestingly, the first Big Ten basketball game he would attend would be the infamous Ohio State at Minnesota brawl a few months later.) "I really had a baptism by fire with Woody," Duke explains. "I had just taken over as commissioner and one of the first things I had to deal with was this." It wouldn't be the last time Duke would have to deal with a controversial game in this rivalry. Two years later, Duke himself would be on the receiving end of a verbal barrage by Bo Schembechler.

After the game, Woody refused to conduct a post-game press conference and a team spokesman emerged from the locker room to inform the media of this.

Earle Bruce explains: "We were all still upset about the call and still surprised at what Woody had done. So not much good would have come from having a post-game press conference. In the next few days, Woody would take a lot of heat from the Ohio State administration for what he had done. Actually, Michigan athletic director Don Canham probably helped Woody out by saying some of the things that he did."

Canham would later mention that a personality like Woody was probably good for an additional 20,000 in ticket sales. "I always had, and still do have, a lot of respect for Woody Hayes," Canham explains. "He was out of line in that particular instance.

But things like that often overshadowed all the good things he did. Not just for his players, but for people everywhere." Canham also remembers Woody later offering to pay for the damage to the sideline markers. "Woody wrote me and offered to pay for whatever he broke. But, of course, I didn't take it. Actually, I personally owned a company that manufactured those markers and we made an ad that featured a picture of Woody tearing them up. We put the caption 'Our yard markers are almost indestructible' under the picture with Woody tearing one apart."

For his part, Bo still thinks Woody's outburst was at least partially premeditated. "I know he was mad," Bo remembers. "But when he was out on the field, I looked right at him and could see that his glasses were all fogged up from the changing weather that day. He was putting on a show so people would forget he was 6-4 and would only remember his protest. He was setting up the 1972 game. People tell me I'm nuts to say that, but you just had to know him and how smart he was. He was very calculating. Even now, people talk more about his outburst than they do about the fact that he lost."

Michigan would go on to lose the Rose Bowl to Stanford on a last second field goal and finish the year ranked #6. Ohio State went back to Columbus where they immediately began feverishly planning for the 1972 game.

Woody took some flack for his tantrum, but eventually the attention it received died down. A few seasons later, Woody ran into to Jerry Markbreit and the two decided to send autographed copies of their books to each other. "I always liked Woody and he sent me a copy of *You Win with People*, which I still have in my office," Markbreit explains. "When I opened it up, the signature read, 'To Jerry Markbreit. A great referee . . . but not always.' He was great."

#3 **MICHIGAN**	**10**
OHIO STATE	**7**

The Game 1971 — Ann Arbor, Michigan

	Michigan	Ohio State
Total Yards	334	138
Rushing Yards	288	78
Passing Yards	46	60
First Downs	20	7

Key Individual Stats:

BILLY TAYLOR — 25 carries, 125 yards, 1TD

GLENN DOUGHTY — 16 carries, 72 yards

ED SHUTTLESWORTH — 16 carries, 55 yards

TOM CAMPANA — 5 punt returns, 166 yards, 1TD

THE GAME 1972

THE 1972 GAME WAS GOING TO HAVE TO BE VERY SPECIAL if it was going to live up to all the drama of the first three editions of the Ten Year War, and it didn't disappoint. Today, it is still mentioned as a college football classic and it's best known for two great goal line stands. It's not very often that a defense gets to stop an opponent on the brink of the end zone, and it's unheard of for it to happen twice in the same game. There has probably never been a better display of short yardage and goal line defense by anyone, anytime, anywhere. The fact that there was so much riding on the game made it that much more unbelievable.

The NCAA and the Big Ten had both made changes before the season that would forever alter the Michigan-Ohio State series. Freshmen were granted eligibility by the NCAA, and the "no-repeat" Rose Bowl policy was repealed by the Big Ten conference. Freshman players like Archie Griffin, Ken Kuhn, and Tim Fox made an impact at Ohio State while Michigan would be eligible for the Rose Bowl, even though they had gone the previous year. These changes would add to the excitement of the 1972 game.

After a disappointing rebuilding year in 1971, Woody Hayes had reloaded. All the injuries that had occurred during the 1971 season forced Woody to give many underclassman a lot of playing time, and that experience would pay dividends for the next few years. During the second game of the season, against North Carolina, a freshman running back named Archie Griffin made his debut and set the single-game rushing record at Ohio State with 239 yards. For the season, Griffin and fullback Champ Henson combined to run for almost 1,500 yards, and Henson was the nation's leading scorer with 19 touchdowns heading into the Michigan game.

Junior Greg Hare, a very good option runner, won the quarterback job and he ably led the Ohio State offense. With Griffin's emergence, Rick Galbos moved to wingback and was the Buckeyes' leading pass catcher. John Hicks, Jim Kregel, Merv Teague, Chuck Bonica, and Steve Myers made up a big, athletic offensive line. The offense was effective as Hare, Griffin, and Galbos threatened the flanks of a defense while fullbacks Henson and Randy Keith pounded inside.

The Ohio State defense endured several injuries throughout the year but had solidified into a good unit by the Michigan game. George Hasenohrl, Jim Cope, Pete Cusick, and Shad Williams were very strong as a defensive line while All-American Randy Gradishar led a great group of linebackers that included Rick Middleton and Vic Koegel. Neal Colzie was the premiere player in a good secondary that suffered numerous injuries throughout the year.

The Buckeyes opened their season with seven straight wins and had climbed as high as #5 in the AP poll before losing at Michigan State 19-12. Ohio State rebounded the following week to beat Northwestern and were ranked #9 heading into the game against Michigan. If they could defeat the Wolverines, they would be co-champions with Michigan and would go to the Rose Bowl to face #1 USC.

Despite losing several key players from the Rose Bowl team of 1971, Bo had assembled one of his best teams in 1972. The Michigan program was now to the point where their success on the field fed their recruiting program, which, in turn, led to more success. This cycle of the rich getting richer was what separated Michigan and Ohio State from the rest of their conference peers; from 1968-1980, only the Buckeyes or Wolverines represented the Big Ten in Pasadena.

Michigan won primarily with defense as the Wolverines had only allowed 43 points through their first ten games and led the nation in defense against the score. Fred Grambau and Dave Gallagher were the anchors up front while Craig Mutch and Tom Kee led a stout linebacking corps. All-American wolfman Randy Logan and safety Dave Brown were the backbone of one of the best secondaries in the country. The Michigan defense ranked #4 nationally in total defense by allowing only 218 yards per game.

Sophomore quarterback Dennis Franklin gave the Michigan offense an added threat with his running ability and was a good passer when called upon. His receiving targets included mammoth tight end Paul Seal, wingback Clint Haslerig, and split end Bo Rather. But, like all great Michigan and Ohio State teams, the strength of the offense was a punishing running game. Tailbacks Chuck Heater and Harry Banks were solid runners as were fullbacks Bob Thornbladh and leading rusher Ed Shuttlesworth. They all found running room behind a great offensive line that included All-American tackle Paul Seymour, along with Jim Coode, Mike Hoban, Bill Hart, and Tom Coyle.

Michigan routed a highly ranked UCLA team at Los Angeles early in the year and, the week before the Ohio State match-up, beat Purdue 9-6 on a Mike Lantry field goal late in the game. The

Wolverines rolled through their schedule undefeated and would enter "The Game" 10-0 and ranked #3.

Due to the new Big Ten rule, Michigan would be the first team in conference history to be eligible for consecutive Rose Bowls as Big Ten champion. As was normal during the Ten Year War, the Michigan-Ohio State winner would head to Pasadena.

Both teams had their share of injuries entering the week of the game. Michigan fullback Ed Shuttlesworth had injured his ankle and, although he would play, it wasn't completely healed by game time. Ohio State was even more banged up as linebacker Vic Koegel and defensive back Lou Mathis would both miss the Michigan game. Their replacements, Arnie Jones and Doug Plank, would both play pivotal roles in one of the most memorable defensive performances in Buckeye history. Randy Gradishar had also hurt his knee but would play and play very well against the Wolverines.

Woody and Bo kept mostly quiet before the game, although Bo hinted during a press conference that, since Michigan had already clinched a share of the conference championship, he might play for a tie if the opportunity presented itself. A tie would give Michigan the outright title and the Rose Bowl birth, and Bo commented that these things would enter into his thinking if the game unfolded that way. During the game, however, Bo's competitive nature took over and he repeatedly shunned playing for a tie.

One piece of bulletin board material that made it into the Ohio State locker room was a quote attributed to Michigan quarterback Dennis Franklin. Kaye Kessler of the *Columbus Citizen-Journal* noted that when asked why so many Ohio high school players were on the Michigan roster, Franklin, a Massillon native, said, "All Ohio football players don't go to Michigan, only the good ones." Like most years, Michigan was loaded with players from the Buckeye state in 1972. Franklin's quote, though said jokingly, was frequently mentioned during the season and really received a lot of attention during the week of the game.

During Michigan Week, Woody Hayes liked to bring back former players to speak to his team about what "The Game" meant to them. One of those speakers in 1972 was former defensive lineman Dave Whitfield.

Archie Griffin recalls Whitfield's speech. "Whitfield started telling us how much the Michigan game meant to him and he started getting emotional. At the end of his speech, he finished with the words: 'This isn't a football game! This is war!'

"As I looked around the room, I saw several other people crying as well. And that's when the importance of the game really hit me. I was born at University Hospital and raised and played high school football in Columbus. I thought I understood the Michigan rivalry, but I didn't until that day. Seeing grown men and my teammates getting so emotional days before a game really made it hit home. I've never forgotten that."

Saturday brought dark skies, rain showers, and cold temperatures in the 30s. But the capacity crowd at Ohio Stadium started loud and got louder as the day progressed. Both teams, as usual, were at an emotional peak for the game as each charged out of their locker rooms in a frantic release of emotions. It was obvious that Woody and Bo had again whipped their players into a state of frenzy.

Michigan received the opening kickoff and promptly marched into Ohio State territory. Dennis Franklin started out hot by hitting passes to Bo Rather and Larry Gustafson, and ran well on option plays and scrambles. The Wolverines faced a third-and-one situation at the OSU 31 and shot themselves in the foot with a procedure penalty. With the five-yard mark-off, Michigan was forced to pass and Arnie Jones sacked Franklin back at the 45 yard line. It was the first of many drives that began well for Michigan but would end without points as the Ohio State defense stiffened when they neared their end zone.

Ohio State was unable to move the ball on their first drive, and Michigan got the ball back at the UM 44. Franklin stayed sharp, hitting Clint Haslerig for one first down and then passing to tight end Paul Seal on a delay pass to set up a fourth-and-two at the OSU 32. Franklin then gained three yards and a first down on an option run. The Wolverines were in scoring position. Once again, however, the Buckeye defense tightened, stuffing two running plays and forcing an incompletion on third down. Mike Lantry was brought in to attempt a 44-yard field goal, which was no good. The score remained 0-0.

On their next possession, Ohio State again failed to gain a first down as Greg Hare was drilled a yard short by Dave Brown on an option play. Gary Lago punted to the UM 33, but Brown was hit as he was attempting a fair catch and Ohio State was penalized 15 yards. The penalty gave Michigan great field position at their 48 yard line. As the first quarter wound down, the Wolverine offense kept up the pressure. Franklin ran for 10 yards and tailback Chuck Heater ran through a huge hole up the middle for 19 more.

For the third straight time, the Ohio State defense wouldn't break. The drive stalled at the OSU 18. Kicker Mike Lantry gave Michigan a 3-0 lead with a 35-yard field goal on the third play of the second quarter.

"We were frustrated that we couldn't score more, but we felt good about what we were doing," Dennis Franklin remembers. "We moved the ball very well three times in row and felt like we were controlling the game. But in a game of this magnitude, you'd better make the most of your opportunities."

On the ensuing possession, the Buckeye offense finally showed some signs of life after going three-and-out of their first two drives. On first down, Hare ran left on a perfect option play for 19 yards. As he was tackled out of bounds, several Michigan players went into the Ohio State bench with him and Woody Hayes was knocked down. There was some pushing and shoving for a moment before everyone was separated, but the play seemed to give the Buckeyes a little spark. They crossed midfield on a Champ Henson plunge on a fourth-and-inches play before being stopped and forced to punt. Lago's kick was downed at the UM 5 yard line. If the defense could hold, then Ohio State would get the ball back in good field position.

That's exactly what happened as Michigan again hurt themselves with a penalty on a third-and-one play. The Wolverines couldn't convert on third-and-six, and were forced to punt out of their own end zone.

Neal Colzie returned the kick to the UM 46, and Ohio State was set up in great position. Archie Griffin took an option pitch for ten yards, then fullback Randy Keith ran twice for eight more. The Michigan defense committed their own costly penalty by jumping offsides on third-and-two, giving the Buckeyes a first down at the UM 22 yard line. Griffin then had an excellent 18-yard run as he went off right tackle and followed fullback Randy Keith downfield before finally being tackled at the Michigan 4.

With the crowd going crazy, Ohio State lined up in the full house backfield. Fullback Champ Henson plunged straight in the line twice before punching it in on third-and-goal from the 1 yard line. It was Henson's 20th touchdown of the year and, as Ohio State fans showered the field with rolls of toilet paper, Blair Conway kicked the extra point to give the Buckeyes a 7-3 lead with 4:30 left in the first half.

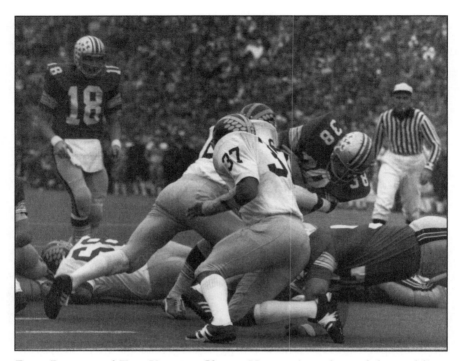

Dave Brown and Tom Kee stop Champ Henson just short of the goal line. But on the next play, Henson would blast into the end zone for a touchdown.

After the kickoff, Michigan started at their 20 yard line and continued to move the ball against the Ohio State defense. Haslerig picked up nine yards on a wingback sweep, and then Franklin hit Paul Seal for 35 yards on a great play-action pass as the big tight end rumbled all the way down to the OSU 36. Two more runs gained another first down, and then Franklin passed for 14 yards to Haslerig to the 11. Chuck Heater then went off right tackle for 10 more yards down to the Ohio State 1 yard line.

Michigan had moved the ball up and down the field against Ohio State, and with a first-and-goal from the 1, it was a foregone conclusion that the Wolverines would punch it in to take a 10-7 halftime lead. On first down, Heater took an option pitch and was dropped for a one-yard loss. Heater got that yard back on a toss play that he cut back into the middle on second down.

Defensive end Van DeCree recalls the crowd's reaction before third down. "I have never in my life heard a crowd like that. After stopping them on the first two downs, I think the fans could feel that we had a shot at stuffing them. They were awesome. The fans just made so much noise. It was unbelievable. As a player in a situation like that, you can feed off that energy. And we did."

On third down, fullback Bob Thornbladh put his head down and rammed into the middle of the Ohio State defense. He gained half a yard before being chopped down by Arnie Jones, Rick Middleton, and Randy Gradishar.

Now, the Wolverines called a timeout to stop the clock with 11 seconds left in the half. Bo Schembechler had a decision to make. Should he go for it from only several inches out, or should he take the almost automatic field goal and go into halftime down only 7-6?

"That wasn't a difficult choice in my mind," Bo remembers. "From that close, you need to punch it in. You don't knock heads all the way down the field to kick from so close. We needed to get it into the end zone."

Michigan broke the huddle and got into the power-I formation as Ohio State dug into their goal-line defense opposite them. At the snap, the ball bounced out of Franklin's hands as he moved from center. He had to fall on the ball at the 2 yard line. The Buckeye defense had held for four straight plays and the celebrating players charged off the field to the deafening cheers of their fans.

"I still get excited when I think about that," Decree recalls. "We did it!"

It was impossible to know at the time, but Ohio State would "do it" again later in the game.

The Ohio State defense celebrates stopping Michigan on fourth-and-goal at the end of the first half. Photo Courtesy of Brockway Sports Photos.

Ohio State ran out the final few seconds of the second quarter, taking a 7-3 lead and a huge dose of momentum into the locker room with them.

Offensive lineman John Hicks remembers what the feeling was for the Buckeye offense at halftime. "We had moved the ball well enough to score, but not as consistent as we wanted. With the way our defense was playing, we felt like if we could get some more points, we'd be in good shape."

Despite out-gaining Ohio State by a huge margin, the Michigan players and coaches were frustrated at being behind.

"We moved the ball up and down the field," offensive line coach Jerry Hanlon remembers. "We knew we had to be sharper once we got into scoring position, but we were confident that we could keep moving the ball."

The Ohio State offense came out after halftime and kept the momentum going by putting together their best drive of the day. After an offsides penalty on Michigan, Archie Griffin carried the ball three straight times to put the ball at the OSU 35. On the next play, quarterback Greg Hare ran the option to the short side of the field. He faked a pitch to Galbos and slithered though the grasp of linebacker Carl Russ at the line of scrimmage. Hare then ran through an arm tackle by Randy Logan at the 40 and cut outside where he stepped over a diving attempt at his legs. He raced down the sideline before finally being knocked out of bounds at the Michigan 30 yard line by Barry Dotzauer and Roy Burks.

The excellent 35-yard run by Hare brought the crowd to their feet and the following play sent them into pandemonium.

Griffin took the ball through a gaping hole in the middle before juking Dave Brown at the 20 and cutting outside for a 30-yard touchdown run.

Greg Hare's 35-yard option run set up Archie Griffin's touchdown on the following play. PHOTO COURTESY OF BROCKWAY SPORTS PHOTOS.

Offensive line coach Ed Ferkany remembers Griffin's run. "It was an isolation play, and Michigan was in a 5-2 defense and slanted their line. We double-teamed the middle guard, and their defensive end didn't slant properly. That enabled our fullback, Randy Keith, to kick out on their outside linebacker. Archie beat their safety and was off to the races."

Wolverine safety Dave Brown also remembers the play. "In my years at Michigan, I can only remember missing one tackle and that's it. You can't make a mistake against a great back like Archie Griffin, or he'll make you pay."

Blair Conway kicked the extra point and Ohio State led 14-3 early in the third quarter.

Michigan had gone from potentially taking a 10-7 lead to being down 14-3 in the span of only a few minutes of play. Now facing an 11-point deficit on the road, the Wolverines needed points immediately. Chuck Heater helped the cause by returning the ensuing kickoff 40 yards to the Michigan 42 yard line. The offense mixed off-tackle runs by Heater, fullback dives by Shuttlesworth and Thornbladh, Franklin option keepers, and a 9-yard pass play to move the ball to the OSU 5.

After three plays gained 4 yards, Michigan was again faced with a fourth-and-goal inside the Ohio State 1 yard line. Being behind by 11 points also meant that there was no discussion about kicking this time at all. On fourth down, Ed Shuttlesworth barreled over right guard Tom Coyle into the end zone, and Michigan was now down 14-9.

Despite the struggles deep in OSU territory, Bo decided to go for the two-point conversion to pull within three points. Dennis Franklin rolled right and fired a pass to Clint Haslerig in the end zone to make the score 14-11 with 4:48 remaining in the third quarter.

Ohio State couldn't get a first down on their next possession, and they were again flagged for fair-catch interference on the punt. The penalty gave Michigan the ball at the UM 49 yard line.

After two fullback dives, Franklin hit Paul Seal with a 15-yard pass to the Ohio State 29. Two Chuck Heater runs then gained a total of five yards before the third quarter came to a close.

On third-and-five, Franklin rolled to his left, saw some open field, and took off. But Doug Plank shot across the field and belted Franklin down just short of the first down. On fourth down, the Buckeye defense once again rose to the occasion as Rick Middleton stuffed Shuttlesworth behind the line of scrimmage. It was the fourth time Michigan had driven into Ohio State territory and had been denied any points. And it wouldn't be the last.

It was now the turn of the Michigan defense to turn in a big play. On second down, Greg Hare rolled out and lofted a pass toward the sideline that was intercepted by Randy Logan at the OSU 29. Franklin then hit Paul Seal for one first down. Runs by Harry Banks and Bob Thornbladh gained another as Michigan set up a first-and-goal from just outside the Ohio State 4 yard line.

On first down, Banks took an option pitch and gained one yard. Banks then ran straight up the middle for three yards to inside the OSU 1. On third-and-goal from the 1, Banks ran off tackle and was hit right at the goal line by Plank. The referees ruled he was stopped short, but many Michigan partisans disagreed.

"Banks scored. No if's, and's, or but's in my mind. He was over the goal line," Jerry Hanlon insists.

Michigan broadcaster Bob Ufer had similar thoughts and wasn't shy about expressing them over the air. "Aren't they going to raise their hands? He was into the end zone! . . . What do you have to do to score a touchdown down here?"

This set up yet another fourth-and-goal situation from the Ohio State 1 yard line. Down 14-11, a field goal would have tied the game and put the pressure on the Buckeyes since a tie would send Michigan to Pasadena.

But Bo's thoughts were just as they were in the first half. "If you can't knock it in from the one yard line, you don't deserve to win the game. We went for it."

Michigan kicker Mike Lantry understood that philosophy. "As a competitor, I wanted to kick the field goal. It would have tied the game. But I agreed with Bo's call then and I still agree with it now. You have to put it the end zone."

Just as in the first half, Michigan came to the line in a power-I formation and Ohio State dug into their goal line defense. At the snap, Franklin lunged into the line on a quarterback sneak but was hit in the hole and stood up by linebacker Randy Gradishar.

"I came over the guard unblocked and hit him short of the goal line just as he was starting to push forward," Gradishar recalls. "I don't know how I came in that clean, but I did."

On fourth-and-goal in the final quarter, Dennis Franklin is stuffed short of the end zone by linebacker Randy Gradishar #53. Photo courtesy of Brockway Sports Photos.

The rest of the defense also converged on Franklin and, almost miraculously, once again the Buckeyes had stopped Michigan on the threshold of the end zone.

"We were sky high when we ran off that field," Van DeCree remembers. "We had stopped them again. Bo should have kicked a field goal, but I'm sure he thought they would score."

Despite another heroic stand, Ohio State wasn't out of trouble. They couldn't get a first down on their next possession and were forced to punt from their end zone. Michigan got the ball back in excellent field position at the OSU 37. But after three plays netted zero yards, the Wolverines were faced with a fourth-down-and-ten.

"I think I made a mistake there," Bo recalls. "We probably should have tried to pin them deep with a punt, but I thought being stopped again would give them a mental edge. So I decided to go for it."

Shad Williams pressured Franklin, who fired a pass towards Heater that was incomplete. This gave Ohio State possession at the OSU 37 with 5:10 left in the game.

Michigan desperately needed to get the ball back, and the Buckeyes desperately needed to move the ball and take some time off the clock. On second down, Hare threw a pass in the flat to Archie Griffin who broke a tackle by Tom Kee at the line of scrimmage and ran 15 yards to the Michigan 48 yard line. Three plays later, Rick Galbos was stopped short of a first down on an option play, but was hit late out of bounds.

The 15-yard penalty gave Ohio State a crucial first down at the UM 28. Bo came onto the field to argue the call, but to no avail. After three more running plays bled precious time off the clock, the Buckeyes lined up for a 46-yard field goal attempt that was wide left. The Michigan offense regained possession at the 20 yard line with 1:20 remaining and with everything on the line.

After throwing two incompletions, Franklin hit Bo Rather for just under 10 yards on third down and Ed Shuttlesworth got the first down on the next play. Franklin then connected with Rather on consecutive plays for 15 and 14 yards to give Michigan a first down at the OSU 41.

The Ohio Stadium crowd, which had been unbelievably loud all day, now reached deafening noise levels as the game came down to this final drive.

Paul Seal got behind the Buckeye defense on first down, but Neal Colzie batted the ball away at the last second near the 5 yard line. Franklin then rolled left and was tackled inbounds for no gain as the clock continued to roll. With 13 seconds left, Franklin fired a pass out of bounds to stop the clock.

Eager fans believed that was the end of the game and stormed onto the field to dismantle the south goal posts. Police and stadium officials tried to clear the field and even Woody Hayes got into the act. Fearing that Michigan might try a field goal, he was concerned that, with those goal posts destroyed, the referees might allow the Wolverines to kick at the opposite end and they would then have the wind at their backs. Hayes pulled a calf muscle running onto the field to chase off the fans but limped back to the sideline after order was restored.

On fourth-and-ten from the OSU 41, Franklin was flushed from the pocket and sacked by George Hasenohrl with only 6 seconds left on the clock. Once again, the Ohio State defense had risen to the occasion. This one sealed it.

Fans again ran onto the field and had to be removed before the game could be completed.

On the final play, Hare fell on the ball and that was it.

Buckeye fans could finally storm the field and celebrate as Woody received a victory ride on the shoulders of his players.

Rick Galbos remembers the mayhem. "Someone took off with my helmet and one of my shoes. But we were all celebrating so I couldn't have cared less."

Disheartened Michigan players left the field with thoughts of what might have been.

"It really hurts when you have that many opportunities and you don't take advantage of them," Ed Shuttlesworth recalls. "I was frustrated because my injury kept me from contributing as much as I wanted on the goal line."

Tears of joy flowed in the Ohio State locker room.

"It was very emotional after the game," John Hicks remembers. "It was such a wild finish and those two goal line stands were amazing. A game like that takes a lot out of you emotionally."

Woody Hayes, injured muscle and all, was thrilled with the upset win. "Our defense rose to magnificent heights." When Big Ten Commissioner Wayne Duke told Woody that an extra set of goal posts had been kept under the stands, Woody replied jokingly that that information would have saved him a pulled muscle.

Ohio State would go to the Rose Bowl to face #1 USC where they were soundly beaten by a great Trojan team that captured the National Championship. Still, the win over Michigan was one of the sweetest in Buckeye history and the extra bowl practice would serve Ohio State well come the fall of 1973.

Michigan would stay home for the holidays to think about how twice they were less than a yard from a touchdown and how those few feet kept them so far from Pasadena.

#9 OHIO STATE	**14**
#3 MICHIGAN	**11**

The Game 1972 — Columbus, Ohio

	Ohio State	Michigan
Total Yards	192	344
Rushing Yards	177	184
Passing Yards	15	160
First Downs	10	21
Turnovers	1	0
Offensive Plays	44	83

Key Individual Stats:

CHUCK HEATER — 14 carries, 65 yards

DENNIS FRANKLIN — 13-23-160 yards

ARCHIE GRIFFIN — 17 carries, 75 yards, 1 TD

ARNIE JONES — 24 tackles

RICK MIDDLETON — 17 tackles

RANDY GRADISHAR — 15 tackles

THE GAME

1973

W ITH TWO COLOSSAL PERSONALITIES like Woody and Bo competing against each other, it was inevitable that controversy would become an even larger part of a rivalry that had always had plenty. From broken yard markers and bruised media members to berated officials and confiscated camera film, each year of "The Ten Year War" seemed to bring fresh controversy.

But there have been few games that can match the uproar caused by the 1973 game. The game itself was a classic, but what happened in the hours and days after the game became legendary. A firestorm of harsh words, insults, bitterness, accusations, and even threatened legal action erupted that would change the Big Ten Conference forever.

In his column on the Monday before the 1973 game, *Columbus Dispatch* sports editor Paul Hornung related a story about Buckeye fullback Bruce Elia:

> *During the previous Saturday's game against Iowa, a 55-13 Ohio State thrashing, Elia took a shot to the head and was groggy.*
> *When he got to the Ohio State bench, the medical staff began to ask him regular questions like "What's your name?" and "Where are you?" to determine if Elia*

*was all right. "What day of the month is it?" was the
final question from the doctor.*

*Elia thought for a moment, then responded, "Let's
see, 24 minus 7. Yeah, this has to be November 17th."*

November 24th was the date everyone in both programs
had been pointing to all season. All year long, it was obvious
that the two superpowers were on a collision course with each
other.

A very strong argument could be made that the 1973
team was the greatest in Ohio State history. They carried the
#1 ranking for eight straight weeks heading into the Michigan
game. Archie Griffin, Kurt Schumacher, John Hicks, Van DeCree,
Randy Gradishar, Neal Colzie, Pete Cusick, Steve Myers, Tim
Fox, and Tom Skladany would all be voted All-American during
their careers.

With the exception of Michigan, no other team came
within 24 points of the Buckeyes during the regular season. After
watching Ohio State crush his team 56-7 in the season opener,
Minnesota coach Cal Stoll said, "They're no longer 3 yards and a
cloud of dust. They're 12 yards and a mass of humanity!"

Hicks, Gradishar, and Griffin all finished in the top six of
Heisman balloting. Woody hinted that he considered this squad
the equal of his 1969 juggernaut.

Ohio State assistant coach Ed Ferkany said, "That 1973
team probably had the best personnel in OSU history. We had
a great offensive line, great running backs, and the defense was
just unbelievable."

Sophomore quarterback Cornelius Greene guided the
powerful Ohio State offense. Nicknamed "Flam" by his teammates for his flamboyant clothes, Greene beat out senior
co-captain Greg Hare to become the first black quarterback at
OSU. (Interestingly, the 1973 game would be the first game in
NCAA history between two top-five teams with African-American

quarterbacks. Woody Hayes was ahead of the curve in playing and recruiting black athletes during the '50s and '60s, and Bo felt the same as his old mentor.)

Even as a sophomore, Greene was a great ball handler. His speed and quickness made him very dangerous running the option. Although the Buckeyes rarely passed, Greene would occasionally make teams pay for loading up against the run by hitting play-action passes to tight end Fred Pagac (later defensive coordinator at his alma mater), split end Dave Hazel, or wingback Brian Baschnagel.

But the hammer that Ohio State used to bludgeon opposing defenses was a running game that featured Big Ten MVP Archie Griffin and three great fullbacks. Griffin had already set a conference record by rushing for 1,265 yards in the first nine games of the season. And after a knee injury sidelined fullback Champ Henson for the season, Bruce Elia and freshman battering-ram Pete Johnson shared the fullback duties.

This backfield found lots of running room behind one of the best offensive lines in college football history. Tackle John Hicks finished second in the Heisman race and won the Outland and Lombardi Trophies while tackle Kurt Schumacher, center Steve Myers, and guard Jim Kregel were all named All-Conference in '73.

As good as the Ohio State offense was, the defense was even more outstanding. They shut out four opponents and led the nation in scoring defense by allowing a paltry 3.6 points per game heading into the Michigan contest. That number would have been amazingly even lower, but both Indiana and Iowa scored points late in the 4th quarter against Buckeye reserves. Remarkably, the first-string Ohio State defense only surrendered a single touchdown in the first 9 games of the season.

Ohio State had defensive stars at nearly every position. All-American Van DeCree held down one defensive end slot and strongman Pete Cusick anchored the middle of the defensive line. The linebacking corps of Rick Middleton, Vic Koegel, and Randy Gradishar were by far the nation's best and probably one of the best units in Big Ten history. All three senior linebackers made the All-Conference team while Gradishar was selected as an All-American.

The defensive backfield was also strong with Tim Fox, Neal Colzie, Steve Luke, and Dick Parsons. Colzie was an All-Conference selection and was also an outstanding punt returner. The defense was aided by Tom Skladany's high, hanging punts that were seldom returnable.

Michigan, ranked #4, also entered the game undefeated and untied. Like Woody had done at Ohio State, Bo had built Michigan into one of the nation's best programs. Heading into the 1973 Ohio State game, Bo had an amazing 48-6 record as head coach of the Wolverines. Only Navy had come within two touchdowns of the Wolverines all season; and after enduring a rash of injuries early in the year, Michigan continued to improve. After the 14-point win over Navy, Illinois was the only other team to even challenge Michigan leading up to the match-up with Ohio State.

Dennis Franklin was in his second year as starting quarterback and was named All-Big Ten due to his running skills and improved passing. He had two great targets to throw to in tight end Paul Seal and wingback Clint Haslerig. While Griffin received the majority of carries from the tailback position at Ohio State, Michigan used a bevy of backs to wear down their opponents. Gil Chapman, Chuck Heater, and Gordon Bell shared the duties at tailback while All-Big Ten selection Ed Shuttlesworth was the workhorse at fullback.

The offensive line had to be patched together, due to injuries, but had rounded back into good shape heading into the Ohio State game. Left guard Bill Hoban was voted All-Big Ten and along with Chris Tucker, Dennis Franks, Dave Metz, and Jim Coode had evolved into a very good unit by the end of the season. They allowed the Wolverines to rush for an average of over 300 yards per contest entering "The Game."

The Michigan defense was only slightly behind their Buckeye counterparts statistically. Ohio State led the nation in scoring defense; the Michigan defense was second by allowing only 5.8 points per game. They were fifth in the nation in total defense, fourth in pass defense, and led the Big Ten in rushing defense. The front seven were strong with All-American defensive tackle Dave Gallagher anchoring a very good defensive line, while Steve Strinko was a great run-stuffing linebacker. All-American safety Dave Brown teamed with wolfman Don Dufek to form a solid secondary. Former walk-on and Vietnam veteran Mike Lantry was the place kicker and was destined to play a huge roll in both the 1973 and 1974 Michigan-Ohio State clashes.

The week of the game finally arrived much to the excitement of both programs. As both teams racked up win after win, the anticipation of their inevitable collision grew week by week. It was a relief to finally focus on what had been looked to all year.

"Everybody, everywhere has been talking about Ohio State for three weeks. How do you get a team prepared for anything? Now, they can talk about Ohio State because that's next," Bo said.

Michigan granted 675 press credentials for the game, the most in Michigan history at that time.

Randy Gradishar said that "the campus got very tense as the game neared. You could feel there was something different about that week. The intensity was everywhere."

The Michigan players could sense it as well. Dennis Franklin remembers the ferocity of practices that week. "The scout team was fired up and they really gave it to us on Tuesday and Wednesday. They knew it was a huge game and they played like it."

The coaches weren't immune to the hype either. Longtime OSU assistant Esco Sarkkinen summed up the upcoming game as a "hammer-and-anvil-type game." He went on to add that "there is so much at stake. The Big Ten championship, the Rose Bowl, the National Championship, the Heisman, the Lombardi, the Outland, and the Coach of the Year award."

Both head coaches were mostly quiet before the game.

Although when told that Ohio State was a four-point favorite and that most sportswriters felt OSU would win, Bo snapped back. "I've got 100 players that think differently. Who said Ohio State was going to win? Sportswriters? My mother knows more about football than sportswriters."

Woody seemed loose in comparison to previous Michigan games. He joked with reporters during the week and was, as always, good for a quote. He laughingly said, "We'll pass 'em right off the field."

Bo laughed when he was told this and said, "If we don't give up the big pass, we'll be okay. But we're not playing Stanford, you know."

Buckeye quarterback Cornelius Greene had injured his throwing hand the previous week and it hadn't completely healed by Saturday. Therefore, Woody's normal reluctance to throw the football multiplied, especially if Ohio State managed to get ahead in the game.

Game day brought overcast skies and some early morning rain showers. As kickoff approached, the rain stopped but the sky remained gray throughout the day. The then-record crowd of 105,223 arrived early and gave Woody his customary round of boos as he watched his team warm up. Woody relished the reception he received from the Michigan Stadium crowd.

This wasn't the only instance of pre-game gamesmanship.

ABC likes to film both teams as they storm the field before the game. Traditionally, the Ohio State team would run out the tunnel, break left, then mass in front of their sideline piling on each other. On this day, John Hicks led the Buckeyes out of the tunnel and went straight for the Michigan "Go Blue" banner. As Wolverine students held the banner that the Michigan team would run under, the Ohio State players tried to tear it down.

Ohio State players attempt to tear down the M Club's "Go Blue" Banner before the game. PHOTO COURTESY OF THE BENTLEY HISTORICAL LIBRARY, UNIVERSITY OF MICHIGAN.

The Buckeye players piled on the banner and jumped up and down, trying to rip it apart. After a few seconds, they retreated towards their own bench. Obviously, the partisan Michigan crowd went crazy, booing the Buckeyes.

From his perch in the press box, Michigan broadcasting legend Bob Ufer went berserk. "They're tearing down Michigan's coveted M Club banner! They will meet a dastardly fate here for that. They have the audacity, the unmitigated gall to tear down the coveted M banner!"

The Michigan players didn't wait for the banner to get back up. They stormed the field and jumped and cheered on the sidelines before the banner was righted. After a few seconds, the banner was fixed and the Wolverine players ran underneath it.

ABC broadcaster Chris Schenkel said: "I don't think I've ever seen two teams more fired up. They can't wait to get after each other."

For the first several minutes of the game, it was obvious that both teams were affected by nerves from all the hype the match-up had generated.

Ohio State went three-and-out on their first possession after Don Dufek knifed into the backfield on first down to drop Griffin for a six-yard loss. Michigan had great field position following the punt. But two plays later, Gil Chapman was stripped of the ball by Dick Parsons and OSU recovered at their own 40. The tension continued to rattle the players as Corny Greene fumbled a snap during the ensuing possession, and the Buckeyes again had to punt after three plays.

Michigan showed signs of life, when they got the ball back, by cranking out two first downs on Shuttlesworth's blasts up the middle. The Buckeye defense stiffened at midfield, and the two teams traded punts on their next few possessions. The Michigan defense contained Griffin and Elia for the remainder of the first quarter. Despite getting two more first downs, the Wolverine offense couldn't mount a sustained drive against the Ohio State defense.

On the first play in the second quarter, OSU faced third-and-two at their own 28 yard line. Archie Griffin then began having what Michigan radio broadcaster Bob Ufer called "one of the great performances we've seen here at Michigan Stadium." Griffin took a pitchout to the right, cut back to the middle, spun away from the grasp of Walt Williamson and Don Dufek, and ran 38 yards before being tackled by Dave Brown. Hicks, Elia, and tight ends Fred Pagac and John Smurda all made great blocks to spring Griffin on the play. It was the first Buckeye first down of the game and brought the Ohio State offense to life for the rest of the second quarter. Griffin ran for another first down before the drive stalled, and Blair Conway kicked a 31-yard field goal to put Ohio State up 3-0.

Buckeye quarterback Cornelius Greene looks over the Michigan defense. Photo courtesy of Brockway Sports Photos.

Gil Chapman took the ensuing kickoff and ran it all the way back to the OSU 28 yard line. But the return was nullified by a clipping penalty. The nasty clip broke the ankle of kicker Tom Skladany. Schembechler had to be restrained on the sidelines as he tore off his hat and screamed at the officials for making the call. But there was no question that it was a blatant clip.

As Skladany was helped to the bench, Woody Hayes came over to check on his star kicker. "He asked the doctor if I could kick off and the doctor said no," Skladany recalls. "He then asked the doctor if I could punt and the doctor again said no. I had broken my leg and dislocated my ankle. Woody thought that since punting didn't require me to run that I might still be able to do that. But I just couldn't."

After both teams had short possessions that produced no first downs, Ohio State took over at their 45 yard line. Archie Griffin pounded the middle of the Michigan defense with consecutive carries of 6, 7, 7, and 13 yards. Griffin was running like a man possessed. He repeatedly broke tackles and dragged defenders with him for extra yards on almost every play. A few fullback plunges by Pete Johnson and a 9-yard run by Griffin on a third-and-one play set up first-and-goal at the Michigan 5 yard line.

It was time, in Woody's words, "to grind meat." Hayes liked to put his team into the full-house backfield formation in these situations.

"Back then, there was no mystery involved when we got in close." Griffin recalled, "We were going to give the ball to the fullback. We had Champ Henson, Bruce Elia, and Pete Johnson. Everyone knew what was coming. They just couldn't stop it."

On first down, Johnson had a 5-yard touchdown run for the ages. He took the handoff, ran over left tackle, and was met at the 4 by Don Coleman and Dave Elliott. He ran through them and was hit at the 2 by Carl Russ, then Don Dufek. He kept his massive thighs churning, and carried Russ and Dufek into the end zone with him.

After Conway added the extra point, Ohio State had a 10-0 lead.

Michigan ran out the few remaining seconds of the half and went into the locker room down by ten points. Given the fact that the Buckeye defense had only given up four touchdowns all season, many people thought the lead was insurmountable.

Schembechler remembers that no one in the Michigan locker room felt that way. "We knew we could come back," Bo recalls. "Our defense was shouting, 'Just score 11 points and we'll win! They won't score another point.' I knew we had a great shot."

Judging from his second-half play calling, Woody Hayes must have made up his mind at halftime that with a 10-0 lead the Buckeyes needed to go into a shell offensively and let the defense win the game. When you have the best defense in the country, this seems like a safe strategy. But the ultra-conservative offensive philosophy Hayes employed in the second half proved disastrous for Ohio State's goal of a national championship.

Michigan received the ball to start the second half and drove into Ohio State territory. Mixing strong runs up the middle by Shuttlesworth and Chapman with a Franklin-to-Haslerig pass completion, the Wolverines managed to drive to the Buckeye 32 yard line. On second-and-two, Franklin dropped back to pass, hesitated in the pocket for a moment, then threw deep into the end zone for Keith Johnson. Johnson was well covered by three OSU defenders and Neal Colzie picked off the pass, ending the first Michigan scoring threat of the day.

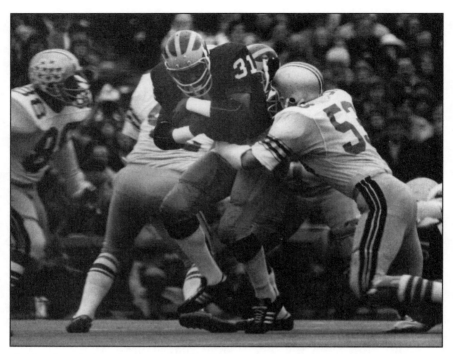

Fullback Ed Shuttlesworth drives into the Ohio State defense early in the third quarter. Shuttlesworth was the workhorse for Michigan, carrying 27 times for 116 yards. PHOTO COURTESY OF THE BENTLEY HISTORICAL LIBRARY, UNIVERSITY OF MICHIGAN.

Despite the Buckeyes getting a first down on several punishing Griffin carries, the teams traded punts on their ensuing possessions. Ohio State took over on their own 40 yard line and started a drive that might have put the game out of reach. On first down, quarterback Cornelius Greene ran a perfect option play for 18 yards down to the Michigan 42. After three running plays gained eight yards, the Buckeyes faced a huge fourth-and-two from the Michigan 34.

Getting a first down would put OSU in field goal range at minimum and may have allowed them to continue on and slam the door shut with a touchdown. With the score already 10-0,

Michigan couldn't allow any more points if they were going to have any chance at coming back.

Greene took the snap, started to run the called option play to the left, noticed the Wolverine defense was slanted that way, then decided to try to cut inside for the two yards. Defensive tackle Jeff Perlinger fought off a block and chopped Greene's legs out from under him after only a one-yard gain.

If any play was the turning point of the game this was it. Woody said after the game, "I really thought we were going on to score a touchdown and maybe put the game out of reach."

As the celebrating Michigan defensive players ran off the field, it seemed that the game's momentum had swung in their favor. Ohio State would not regain that momentum for the remainder of the game.

The defensive stop seemed to invigorate the Wolverine offense. Dennis Franklin hit Haslerig for an 11-yard pass completion, and Ed Shuttlesworth continued to pound the middle of the Buckeye defense for decent yardage. The big fullback carried eight times on the drive that consumed the rest of the third quarter.

On the first play of the fourth quarter, Arnie Jones knifed into the backfield and dropped Gil Chapman for a loss on a third-and-three play from the Ohio State 13 yard line. From there, Mike Lantry kicked a 30-yard field goal and the score was now 10-3 in favor of OSU.

Ohio State went three-and-out on their next possession, and Michigan got the ball back at their own 49 yard line. After yet another Shuttlesworth plunge into the line gained five yards, Franklin threw a strike over the middle to tight end Paul Seal. Seal caught the ball at the OSU 31 and raced down to the 19 yard line. Shuttlesworth, who finished the day with 116 yards, then carried three consecutive times for just over nine yards.

The chains were brought in for measurement to show that Michigan needed two inches for a first down from the Ohio State 9 yard line.

Everyone in the stadium and the millions watching on TV all knew what the play call would be. Schembechler would obviously give the ball to Ed Shuttlesworth and let the big fullback smash into the heart of the Buckeye defense as he had all day.

Dennis Franklin barked out cadence from the power-I formation as he looked over Ohio State's goal line defense. At the snap, Franklin faked a handoff to Shuttlesworth who drew most of the Buckeye defenders, then ran an option play around the right side of the line. Franklin cut inside of Neal Colzie at the line of scrimmage and scampered into the end zone untouched.

The partisan Michigan Stadium crowd erupted into pandemonium. The touchdown was a perfect call that was executed brilliantly.

"I knew they would be keying on Shuttlesworth. That's why we went to Franklin," Bo said.

Mike Lantry kicked the extra point and the score was now 10-10 with 9:32 left in the game.

With the score now tied, Woody stuck to his game plan and Archie Griffin continued his amazing performance. After a five-yard run on first down, Griffin ran off left tackle for 13 yards, breaking tackles and spinning for extra yardage. With Michigan sticking eight men at the line of scrimmage, Hayes continued to call Griffin's number. The sophomore tailback gained four more yards on his next carry, then got seven more over left tackle before being tackled by Dave Brown and twisting his knee.

As Griffin hobbled off the field, Elmer Lippert took his place and gained four yards in two carries. Facing third-and-six from the Michigan 47 yard line, Ohio State took a timeout and then put Archie Griffin back in the game. Griffin got the call again but was tackled for only a three-yard gain by Steve Strinko. This brought on fourth-and-three.

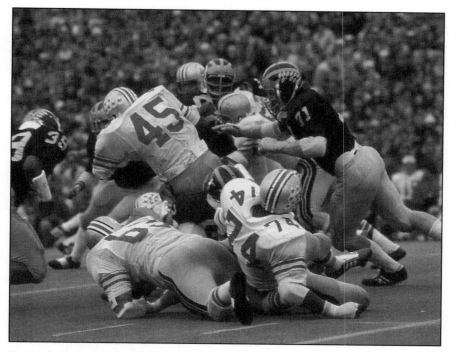

Even though the Michigan defense was stacked against him, Archie Griffin still rushed for an amazing 163 yards on 30 punishing carries. Photo Courtesy of Brockway Sports Photos.

The Buckeyes would have to punt the ball back to Michigan.

Some Ohio State players and coaches couldn't understand Woody's ultra-conservative play calling at this point in the game.

Offensive assistant Ed Ferkany recalls the frustration that had set in. "Woody really buttoned up the offense in the second half. We ran no wide plays and didn't vary our attack enough. It's hard to run against a team like Michigan when they've got everyone wedged at the line of scrimmage. They kept bringing their safety up, creating an eight- or nine-man front and dared us to throw the ball. We didn't."

The Ohio State offensive coaches continued to lobby Woody to run a counter or an option play or a wingback reverse. But Hayes was having none of that.

As these plays were mentioned, Woody would shake them off and say: "F— that! We're not running that f—ing play."

Despite the pleas from his assistants, Woody continued to send Griffin straight into the middle of the Michigan defense.

Quarterback coach George Chaump also recalls being upset. "Woody went into a shell offensively. That was just his nature. We knew we needed to open things, but he wouldn't do it."

Michigan got the ball back on their own 11 yard line. Dennis Franklin continued to be hot, hitting Haslerig for gains of 14 and 15 yards. On second-and-five from the Michigan 44 yard line, Franklin dropped back to pass and released the ball just as

Dennis Franklin hands off to Gil Chapman. PHOTO COURTESY OF BROCKWAY SPORTS PHOTOS.

Buckeye defensive end Van DeCree was bearing down on him. Ed Shuttlesworth caught the pass for a 7-yard gain, but DeCree crushed Franklin as he let go of the ball. Franklin didn't get up from the hit.

"I knew Dennis from high school," Decree says. "I said, 'Dennis, get up, man.' But he held his shoulder and said, 'I can't.' He hung in there and completed the pass. You have to respect that."

The hit by Decree ended Franklin's season and contributed to a vote that would ignite a huge controversy and change the Big Ten's bowl policy.

Larry Cipa replaced Dennis Franklin at quarterback for the Wolverines. Cipa had also come off the bench in the 1971 game after Tom Slade had been injured, and he lead Michigan to a come-from-behind 10-7 win. Shuttlesworth carried on both first and second downs, and gained 7 yards to set up a third-and-three from the OSU 42 yard line. Shuttlesworth again got the call but was dropped, after only getting a yard, by Pete Cusick and Randy Gradishar.

Facing fourth-and-two from the Buckeye 41 with 1:06 left in the game, Bo called a timeout to ponder his options. "I knew Lantry had a great leg. Fifty-eight yards was obviously a lot to ask of any kicker. But there was a little wind behind us and I thought he could make it. We talked it over and decided to try the field goal instead of going for it. Punting never entered my mind. That would have been surrendering to a tie and we felt like we were in control of the game at that point. We thought we were going to win."

At that moment, it would be hard to imagine a bigger kick. Any field goal from any distance would have been huge under the circumstances. But a 58-yard field goal with a minute left, by a walk-on, left-footed, 25-year-old Vietnam veteran with a wife and a baby, would be monumental. If Lantry made it and Ohio

State was unable to answer in the remaining minute, it might well be the most famous field goal in college football history.

As Lantry trotted onto the field, he knew he would have to give it everything he had to get it there.

The snap was perfect. The ball was spotted and held by Larry Gustafson. Lantry swung his sledgehammer leg and drove the ball over the hands of the Buckeye defenders who were desperately trying to block it.

"When it left my foot, I thought I had it," Lantry recalls. "It was headed straight for the inside of the left upright. It just hooked left at the end. Maybe the wind took it a little."

The kick had enough distance and, at first, looked like it would be good. But as the ball neared the goal posts, it hooked left slightly. Despite being long enough, the kick missed by a mere 18 inches to the left.

The Michigan field goal unit left the field assuming that a shot at victory had passed. They had no idea that they would be back out on the field in a few plays to again try a game winning field goal.

After the missed field goal, Ohio State took over at their own 20 yard line with 1:01 left.

The Buckeye offense had run the ball 49 consecutive plays and had yet to even attempt a pass. Greg Hare, who was a better passer than Greene, was inserted into the line-up. With so little time left and Ohio State's hopes of a national championship fading fast, Woody realized that he now HAD to pass.

On first down, Hare dropped back and fired a pass toward the sideline for Brian Baschnagel. Wolverine defensive back Tom Drake cut in front of Baschnagel at the OSU 40 yard line and picked it off. Drake was tackled at the Ohio State 33 yard line with 52 seconds left as Michigan Stadium erupted.

Michigan was already within Lantry's range but obviously wanted to get closer. There was so much pandemonium on the Michigan sideline after the interception that Cipa was unable to get the play into the huddle in time and had to take Michigan's final timeout.

This was crucial because Bo now rushed everything in order to make sure Lantry would still have time to kick without being hurried. Instead of running three or more plays, the Wolverines essentially ran one.

Gil Chapman carried on first down for 6 yards to the Buckeye 27 yard line. As the clock continued to roll, Cipa took the second-down snap and fired a pass out of bounds to stop the clock. Facing third-and-five with 28 seconds to go and no timeouts left, Bo decided that now was the time to try the field goal.

Almost unbelievably, Lantry would now get another chance to win the game with his left foot.

Michigan broadcaster Bob Ufer's voice cracked as he excitedly set the scene: "Here we have the dramatic moment in 1973 Big Ten football. One of the most titanic moments in the history of Michigan football!"

The record crowd all stood on their feet in nervous anticipation.

Archie Griffin, who finished the game with an amazing 163 yards, remembers sitting on the sideline hoping Lantry would miss. "I was exhausted and so nervous that I almost couldn't watch it."

Once again, the snap was good and the Ohio State defenders leaped into the air trying to block the 44-yard attempt. Lantry hit the ball well, and the kick had plenty of distance. But it veered wide right.

"It's possible I compensated for the first kick going left. But I wasn't thinking about that when I kicked it. It just went wide right," Lantry remembers.

Mike Lantry wouldn't be the hero on this day, and he would be in a similar situation in 52 weeks in Columbus.

The score remained at 10-10 and now Ohio State took over at their own 20 yard line with 24 seconds left.

It was desperation time for the Ohio State offense.

With any shot at a national championship and most likely a trip to the Rose Bowl slipping away, Hare was instructed to throw the ball deep. His first-down pass was heaved into Michigan territory and was batted around by two Buckeyes and four Wolverines before finally falling incomplete. His next throw was also a desperation toss and was almost intercepted. With only six seconds left, Hare once again dropped back and heaved a prayer that fell harmlessly out of bounds.

With that, the game was over. The excitement that the game had generated would be matched with controversy over the next few days.

As the players left the field, neither team had a feeling of satisfaction. But the Ohio State players were more dejected. Their #1 ranking was gone, and most felt that Michigan would be sent to go to the Rose Bowl when the Big Ten athletic directors voted on Sunday.

"To me, it felt like a loss," said Van DeCree. "I told my buddy [Michigan defensive lineman] Timmy Davis to have fun at the Rose Bowl."

Archie Griffin remembers having similar thoughts: "Since we had gone the year before, I figured Michigan would get the vote. At the time, I felt like we had lost the game."

Offensive line coach Ed Ferkany said the coaching staff felt the same way: "I knew the no-repeat rule was no longer in effect. But as far as we were concerned, we had lost. We left Ann Arbor with the attitude that they were going to go to Pasadena. We assumed our season was over."

At the post-game press conference, a dejected Woody Hayes summed up his team's feelings. "We knew we had to win this one to go, and we didn't." When asked by reporters why he had refused to attempt even a single pass until the final minute of the game, Hayes snapped back. "We didn't pass because our passing isn't good. It hasn't been good all year."

The Michigan players didn't feel as if they had won the game, but most of them felt that they were on their way to the Rose Bowl.

Safety Dave Brown was quoted, "It isn't as good as a win, but they weren't the best team out there today. Now, we'll go to the Rose Bowl."

Even Bo felt confident. "I have no predictions," Bo said after the game, "but if they vote to send Michigan, we deserve to go. Why? If you have to ask that, then you didn't see the game."

Most people in the Michigan program felt that winning the statistical battle (Michigan had more first downs, 16-9, and total yards, 303-234), the late field goal attempts, and the fact that Ohio State had gone the year before would swing the athletic directors vote in their favor.

Michigan athletic director Don Canham had been one of the prime advocates of doing away with the silly and outdated no-repeat rule the previous year. But the mentality that teams couldn't go in back-to-back years still lingered, especially in a situation like this where two teams tied for the championship and tied on the field. The fact that Wolverine quarterback Dennis Franklin had broken his collarbone was discussed but not considered to be a serious factor in the vote the following day.

Even Dick Otte of the *Columbus Dispatch* said, "The odds look like a zillion to one that the vote will favor Michigan."

If the vote ended in a 5-to-5 tie, Michigan would get the nod based on the Buckeyes' trip out West the previous year.

The next day, the storm broke.

Big Ten Commissioner Wayne Duke conducted the athletic directors' vote by phone on Saturday night and Sunday morning, with the official announcement of the results coming at 1 p.m. that afternoon. When the vote was completed, Duke called Ohio State athletic director Ed Weaver and told him that the vote ended 6-4 in favor of the Buckeyes but to keep it quiet until the official announcement later that day.

Weaver then called Woody and broke the news to the elated coach. He too was sworn to secrecy until the official word came down. Woody promptly called his wife Anne at home, hummed a few bars of "California Here We Come," and hung up. She got the message.

When the official announcement was made, Ohio State players were scattered all over campus. Archie Griffin heard the news when he walked into a meeting where several other players were excitedly talking about the decision. "We were surprised but excited." John Hicks remembers talking with Woody on Sunday morning: "He told us they'd vote for Michigan because he wasn't very popular with the conference brass. So when we found out the vote went our way, we were surprised." Randy Gradishar was driving home from the game when he heard the news: "I had stayed behind after the game and was driving back to Columbus when the news came over the radio. I had thought that I'd played my last collegiate game, so I was thrilled."

Bo Schembechler was at the Channel 4 studio in Detroit getting ready to do his weekly TV show when he received word of the vote. A phone call came in that the athletic directors had chosen Ohio State.

As the word buzzed around the studio, the reporters there all headed to Bo to get his take. "When they told me, I just couldn't believe it. I was enraged and stunned. I thought there had to be some mistake."

The show was cancelled that day as Bo, Michigan sports information director Will Perry, and *Detroit News* sportswriter Jerry Green hopped in a car and headed back to Ann Arbor.

"I kept saying, 'How am I going to tell my team?' I couldn't believe how unfair this was, and I didn't know how I could face my players." When Bo called a team meeting to let his team know what had happened, he was at a loss for words. "I broke down and cried in front of them. I didn't know what to say."

Defensive lineman Tim Davis remembers Bo's speech to the team. "Bo's face was white as a sheet. It was obvious that he was furious and holding back tears at the same time. We had never seen him like that before, and I can still remember the feeling we had as he stood before us. I'll never forget that."

The phones at the Big Ten offices in Chicago became jammed with calls from angry Michigan fans. The local press in Michigan echoed their readers over the next several days with many columns blasting the vote and the way with which it was handled. One Michigan graduate student even went so far as to file a class action suit in federal court to overturn the decision. In the end, the suit was dropped but made for more fodder for the press. Bo threatened to accept another bowl invitation in spite of the conference's bowl ban and even spoke of pulling Michigan out of the Big Ten altogether.

After getting back to Ann Arbor and receiving the official word, Schembechler started his assault. With local and national press buzzing with the news, Bo talked to anyone who would listen. "This is the darkest day of my athletic career. I'm very bitter." Bo then went on to blast the conference and commissioner Wayne Duke. "The Big Ten administration hasn't been very tough, and it hasn't been very good. There were petty jealousies involved in this and I'll be very interested to see how each school voted, particularly our sister school Michigan State."

Duke and the conference athletic directors had decided to not make the final count public and also not to reveal how each

AD had voted. Over the next few days, this ended up helping Bo's cause because the tally and each director's vote became known through the media. The fact that it had tried to be kept secret only gave credence to Bo's charges of corruption. Don Canham of Michigan, Bill Orwig of Indiana, Bump Elliott of Iowa, and Paul Giel of Minnesota all voted for the Wolverines. Ed Weaver of Ohio State, Tippy Dye of Northwestern, George King of Purdue, Cecil Coleman of Illinois, Elroy Hirsch of Wisconsin, and Burt Smith of Michigan State voted for the Buckeyes.

Michigan fans were incensed that the Michigan State athletic director had voted for Ohio State, and Burt Smith's name would be all over Ann Arbor when the two teams played in 1974. Bo said that if Biggie Munn and Duffy Daugherty had still been the AD and head coach at MSU that they would have voted for Michigan "because they're class guys and would have done what's right."

Smith, like all the other athletic directors, mentioned Dennis Franklin's injury when asked why they had voted for the Buckeyes. In the press, Bo called Franklin's injury an excuse. "If it was so important to them, why didn't any of them call our team doctor to check on Franklin's status?" On Monday, Schembechler continued along these lines. "If the quarterback is so important, why is a team going there that admittedly has no passing attack? What if something were to happen to Cornelius Greene in practice before the bowl? Are they going to send Ohio State home? They just used Franklin as a scapegoat. We have a good backup in Larry Cipa who led us to victory over Ohio State in 1971. I want Wayne Duke to come to Ann Arbor and tell my team to their face that they're not good enough to play in the Rose Bowl. I want him to look Larry Cipa in the eye and tell him he's not good enough to quarterback our team in the Rose Bowl." Tom Slade, who quarterbacked the Wolverines in their Rose Bowl after the 1971 season, was also still on the team and was third string behind Franklin and Cipa.

Franklin's injury contributed to the controversy of the vote. Photo Courtesy of Brockway Sports Photos.

Woody Hayes smartly refused to comment on the uproar at first. He humbly said that Ohio State would do their best to make the conference proud. He mentioned that Franklin's injury was probably a factor in the outcome of the vote and noted that the teams tied despite Michigan having a home field advantage. "We played an even game on an uneven field." After several days of being hounded about the vote however, Hayes finally snapped back on Wednesday. "I'm tired of all that talk. This is typical of today where every decision is questioned. I've always accepted decisions and the one, twelve years ago by the Ohio State regents to keep us out of the Rose Bowl, was a pretty hard one to take." While Hayes had accepted the 1961 Rose Bowl refusal by his own administration very well, the statement that he "always accepted decisions" would probably have come as a surprise to referees, unsuspecting cameramen, and a set of first-down markers in Ann Arbor.

Bo felt, and still does over thirty years later, that Wayne Duke lobbied the athletic directors on Ohio State's behalf. "I had talked with Illinois coach Bob Blackmon on Saturday evening," Bo said. "He said that Cecil Coleman was voting for us. Then, after a phone call from Duke, he changes his mind and votes for Ohio State on Sunday. I've heard from other directors that Duke mentioned Dennis Franklin's injury as he was polling them. He was worried that the Big Ten had lost the past few Rose Bowls and he was running scared. He tried to push the vote in Ohio State's favor."

For his part, Wayne Duke has always categorically denied orchestrating or influencing the vote in any way. "Totally absurd," Duke said of the allegations when asked about them a few days after the vote, and he used the exact same words thirty years later. "The charges that I influenced the vote are totally absurd. Bo and I are friends, but I know he still doesn't believe me. But I absolutely did not try to sway the vote at all. I think the athletic directors voted based on which team they thought was the most representative. The policy was in place. I was only the conduit of the ADs' choice. I tallied the votes, and then I bore the brunt."

That "brunt" was the fury of Schembechler, Michigan fans, and the press. Most people outside of Ohio and Michigan didn't disagree as much with the choice as much as the way it was made.

Within a few years, the Big Ten would wisely implement a tie-breaking formula that would take the decision out of the hands of the athletic directors. The sympathy for a 10-0-1 Michigan team that would stay home for the holidays also led to a repeal of the policy that kept teams from playing in any bowl game other than the Rose Bowl.

"We had been working on lifting the bowl ban for a year or so," Duke said. "When I was commissioner of the Big Eight, we had gotten rid of the bowl ban for any other bowl besides the Orange. When I became Big Ten commissioner in 1971, I also wanted to do that here. That 1973 Michigan-Ohio State game certainly helped."

Bo was careful to make it known that he had no issue with Ohio State. "I want to make one thing perfectly clear. Nothing I say has to do with Ohio State. I think they're a tremendous team."

Still, the fervor of the rivalry grew to even greater heights. As Schembechler and the Michigan faithful fumed, Ohio State fans knew that this would make "The Game" in 1974 that much bigger.

Ohio State went on to blast USC in the Rose Bowl 42-21 to finish the year ranked #2. This was redemption for the trouncing the Buckeyes had taken from the Trojans the previous year.

"We promised Woody that we would win that game," John Hicks said. The big win also made the Ohio State players feel like they had justified the faith that the athletic directors had put in them. "After all the uproar, it was very satisfying to go out there and win the Rose Bowl," Brian Baschnagel recalls. "It really felt like we had proven that we deserved to go."

Michigan ended up ranked #6. Bo Schembechler, while still bitter about the vote, tries to see the good that came from the entire episode. "We took the power to choose who goes to Rose Bowl out of the hands of the athletic directors. And, more importantly, we were the driving force in getting more teams into bowls. There were some good things that came out of it, but we paid a terrible price. And I'm still bitter. I told myself that if I ever got over that, I would be doing an injustice to those players. So it still makes me upset, and it will continue to, as long as I live."

#1 OHIO STATE	10
#4 MICHIGAN	10

The Game 1973 — Ann Arbor, Michigan

	Michigan	Ohio State
Total Yards	303	234
Rushing Yards	204	234
Passing Yards	99	0
First Downs	16	9

Key Individual Stats:

ARCHIE GRIFFIN — 30 carries, 163 yards

ED SHUTTLESWORTH — 27 carries, 116 yards

DENNIS FRANKLIN — 7-11-99 yards

THE GAME 1974

IF THE 1973 GAME SET THE BAR for tense, defensive struggles that were decided by the kicking game, then the 1974 contest raised that bar to an all-time high. It would be hard to imagine a more physical, bone-crunching, emotionally draining game than the one played in Ohio Stadium on November 23, 1974. And after all the big hits and paint-swapping had taken place, the outcome was decided by two former walk-on kickers: one, a Czechoslovakian refugee; and the other, a 26-year-old Vietnam veteran with a wife and son.

Woody Hayes had once again put together one of the best teams in college football. After suffering a heart attack in June, Woody lost weight and focused on being ready for the football season as Bo had done in 1970. Cornelius Greene was back to run the fast-break Ohio State offense and had greatly improved his passing skills from the previous year. Archie Griffin was the backbone of the Buckeye attack and was on his way to the first of two Heisman Trophy awards. Griffin would break his own Big Ten rushing record and was in the middle of his NCAA record streak of 31 consecutive games with over 100 yards rushing. Fullbacks Champ Henson and Pete Johnson split playing time; either one was perfect for running over people and creating holes for Griffin.

The offensive line of Kurt Schumacher, Scott Dannelley, Ted Smith, Steve Myers, and Dick Mack was very strong with Schumacher, Mack, and Myers landing on the All-Big Ten team. Tight end Doug France, wingback Brian Baschnagel, and receivers Dave Hazel and Lenny Willis didn't have many passes thrown their way; but they were exceptional when called upon.

The defense wasn't as strong as the previous season due to injuries, but had matured into a solid unit. Pete Cusick and All-American Van DeCree were strong up front while Bruce Elia and Arnie Jones led a very good group of linebackers. Despite being particularly hard hit by injuries, the secondary came together as the season wore on as All-American Neal Colzie, Tim Fox, Doug Plank, and Steve Luke formed a very good unit. Sophomore punter Tom Skladany helped the defense with his howitzer punts, and walk-on placekicker Tom Klaban had emerged as a weapon with his foot. That foot would be worth its weight in gold after the 1974 game.

Michigan, too, was simply reloading. The 1974 Wolverines were led by their defense. Dan Jilek, Jeff Perlinger, Tim Davis, and Greg Morton were a ferocious defensive line and linebackers Larry Banks, Steve Strinko, Carl Russ, and Calvin O'Neal cleaned up anything after that. Safety Dave Brown was an All-American, and he teamed with wolfman Don Dufek and cornerbacks Harry Banks and Tom Drake to form a spectacular secondary. Michigan led the nation in rushing defense, was second in points allowed, and was third in total defense.

One of the reasons the Wolverine defense was so strong was that the offense kept the other team off the field. Quarterback Dennis Franklin was now a senior and was dangerous both running and passing the ball. Chuck Heater moved to fullback where he rushed for 660 yards and opened holes for a great tandem of tailbacks. Gordon Bell and Rob Lytle alternated at tailback to keep each other fresh and had combined to gain over 1,700 yards entering the Ohio State game.

Pat Tumpane, Dave Metz, Jim Armour, Dennis Franks, Kirk Lewis, and Steve King formed a great offensive line that made all those rushing yards possible. Tight end Greg DenBoer, wingback Gil Chapman, and split end Jim Smith gave Franklin plenty of targets to throw to. Kicker Mike Lantry was back again and would once again play a major roll in the outcome of the game.

Both teams had rolled through most of the season without facing much of a challenge. Michigan struggled against both Wisconsin and Illinois, but they won both of those games to come into the Ohio State contest 10-0 and ranked #3 in the country. Ohio State had cruised through the first 8 games of the year ranked #1 and winning by an average score of 45-9.

But everything came crashing down in East Lansing, Michigan, on November 9th in one of the wildest finishes in college football history.

The Buckeyes had built a 13-3 lead in the fourth quarter only to see a 44-yard TD pass and an 88-yard TD run put them behind 16-13 with only a few minutes left. The Ohio State offense desperately drove down the field as the seconds ticked away. Champ Henson was stopped just short of the goal line with only seconds left as the Buckeye players tried to get off a final play before time ran out.

The ball was snapped as the clock hit 0:00, and Brian Baschnagel picked up the loose ball and dove into the end zone. One official signaled touchdown as two others waved him off. Players from both teams celebrated as if they had won while the fans stormed the field.

No one was certain who had been victorious as the teams went to their locker rooms. After 45 minutes had passed, the officials decided that Ohio State hadn't gotten their final play off in time and declared Michigan State the winner.

When Big Ten Commissioner Wayne Duke went into the Buckeye locker room to tell Woody Hayes the news, Woody went ballistic. After several extremely heated moments, cooler heads eventually prevailed but the effects from the loss lingered.

After beating Iowa the following week, Ohio State climbed up to #4 in the AP poll and would face Michigan for a Rose Bowl birth and a shot at a national championship against Southern Cal.

As usual, the week of the game brought the most physical practices of the year, and the hype surrounding the game kicked into overdrive.

Michigan defensive lineman Tim Davis remembers how Bo used different tactics to motivate each player. "I was from Warren, Ohio. And coming out of high school, Ohio State had looked at me and felt I was too small to play in the Big Ten. So when I decided to go to Michigan, Bo would always remind me of that during the Ohio State week. He'd say things like 'Why did I recruit you? You're way too small to be playing against Ohio State. They'll probably run over you all day.' He knew it would get me fired up and he was a master motivator."

Bo wasn't the only one from the Michigan program whose words generated extra incentive for the game. Archie Griffin recalls some remarks that made their way onto the Ohio State bulletin board. "They had the Banks brothers on defense and Larry Banks had told a reporter that if I gained 100 yards rushing, it would be over his dead body. Well, when that was posted in our locker room, it really fired up our offensive linemen. They rightfully took pride in my 100-yard game streak, and those guys looked at those comments as a personal challenge. Of course, Coach Hayes made sure it received plenty of attention."

Woody Hayes also heard Bo mention in a press conference that he thought that the outcome of the contest might be determined in the kicking game. That comment drove Woody to spend a lot of extra practice time working on kicking drills. The fruits of all this extra work would be obvious during the game.

Ohio State was being billed as a slight favorite, but most agreed with Woody when he said the game would be a toss-up. Michigan was riding a 21-game unbeaten streak. Their last loss was at Columbus in 1972.

The game kicked off under very sunny skies and a warm 60 degrees. Michigan's defense lived up to its billing on the first series as they pushed Ohio State back five yards. Cornelius Greene look nervous as he almost fired an interception on the first play of the game and was then sacked on the next play. Due to the defensive stop, Michigan started in excellent field position at their own 47 yard line.

Three running plays gained a first down at the OSU 42. On the next play, Dennis Franklin faked a handoff to Chuck Heater and fired a pass over the middle to speedster Gil Chapman. Chapman caught the ball at the 25, broke a tackle by a diving Doug Plank at the 20, and raced for the corner of the end zone. Tight end Greg DenBoer blocked Tim Fox just long enough downfield to keep Fox from getting to Chapman before he reached the end zone. Fox fought off the block well and tackled Chapman as he was crossing the goal line.

Gil Chapman remembers seeing daylight and turning on the jets. "Once I got into the open field, I just cut outside and ran for the corner with everything I had." Chapman was mobbed by his teammates as they celebrated the touchdown.

Mike Lantry kicked the extra point and just like that Michigan led 7-0.

Ohio State came right back after the touchdown and put together a sustained drive into Michigan territory. After a pass interference penalty gave the Buckeyes a first down, Archie Griffin ran for 18 yards on an option play to the right. Three straight running plays gave Ohio State another first down at the Michigan 33. The drive ended two plays later when Harry Banks and Jeff Perlinger sandwiched Greene on an option keeper, and Greene fumbled. Steve Strinko recovered for the Wolverines at the 26 yard line.

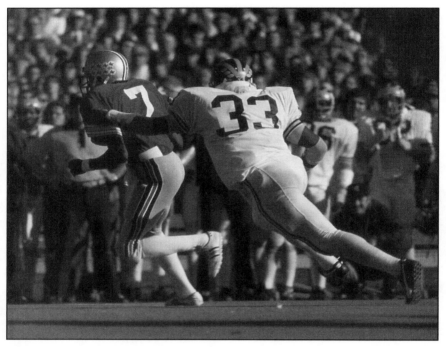

Carl Russ chases Cornelius Greene on an option play. Photo Courtesy of Brockway Sports Photos.

Michigan kept up the pressure on the ensuing drive. The running game was gashing holes in the Ohio State defensive front with quick hitting fullback plunges by Heater and the slashing runs of Gordon Bell. Bell was particularly effective as he carried seven times in the drive for 43 yards. But the Buckeyes tightened, and after two incomplete passes by Dennis Franklin, the drive stalled. Mike Lantry came in and made a 37-yard field goal to give Michigan a 10-0 lead with 4:57 remaining in the first quarter.

It looked like a rout was possible. But those would be the last points Michigan would score.

Now behind 10-0, the Ohio State offense needed to move the ball to regain some momentum. Greene hit tight end Doug France for a first down at the OSU 40. Then after a Griffin run of 8 yards, Greene gained another first down on a 7-yard option play. Griffin got 15 more yards on two tough runs before the drive was stopped at the Michigan 30 as the first quarter came to a close.

On the first play of the second quarter, Tom Klaban came in to attempt a 47-yard field goal. The snap was low but holder Brian Baschnagel did an excellent job of taking the ball off the ground and getting it set for Klaban. The kick was drilled and would have been good from another 10 yards out. Thanks to a great hold by Baschnagel and the great leg of Klaban, Ohio State was now on the board with the score 10-3.

On their next possession, Michigan again had some success running the football right at the Buckeye defense. After getting one first down behind the running of Heater and Bell, Michigan faced a third-and-six at the UM 44. Franklin dropped back and fired a pass over the middle, but it was picked off by Bruce Elia at the OSU 46 and returned to the Michigan 44 yard line.

On the ensuing drive, Griffin carried the ball seven times for 39 yards. They were tough, punishing carries as Griffin ran over linebacker Steve Strinko on one play and kept the drive alive by running for 8 yards on a fourth-and-four play. The pounding took its toll on Griffin as the intensity on both sides resulted in ferocious collisions.

"I was always glad the Michigan game was the last of the season because I wouldn't have been able to play had we played a game the following week," Griffin recalls. "Those games were just so physical. I had a hip pointer and a deep thigh bruise in

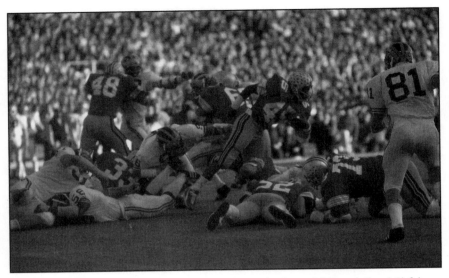

Archie Griffin finds running room through the middle of the Michigan defense. PHOTO COURTESY OF BROCKWAY SPORTS PHOTOS.

that 1974 game. I kept playing, but I could hardly walk the next day. There was some serious hitting in those games on both sides."

Ohio State drove to the Wolverine 7 before the Michigan defense stiffened. Klaban was called on to attempt a field goal. Once again, the snap was bad. And once again, Baschnagel did a great job of getting the ball set for Klaban.

"I wish I could say we practiced for that," Klaban remembers. "But Brian just did a great job of getting the ball down. He was a great athlete and it showed on those two field goals."

The kick was good and Michigan's lead was now 10-6.

After Klaban's second field goal, Michigan came back with a good drive. Gordon Bell continued to gain yards against the Buckeye defense. Mixing runs by Bell and Heater with a Franklin pass completion, the Wolverines reached the OSU 34 where the drive stalled. Lantry attempted a 51-yard field goal into the wind, but it was well short.

With the ball at the OSU 20 and only 1:11 left in the half, most thought Woody Hayes would simply run out the clock and go into halftime down 10-6. But the Ohio State offense gained a few first downs and used their timeouts well. That set up a Cornelius Greene pass to split end Dave Hazel for a 25-yard gain to the Michigan 26.

With 6 seconds on the clock, Klaban came in for his third field goal attempt of the half. Klaban nailed the 43-yard kick, and the half ended with the score 10-9 Michigan.

Tailback Gordon Bell gained 93 yards in the first half and that had the Ohio State coaches upset. "We made some adjustments," Van Decree recalls. "But we just needed to get after it more. They were a great running team, but we really tightened up in the second half."

DeCree's friend from high school, Tim Davis, remembers similar thoughts on the Michigan side. "Griffin was getting some yards on us, but we would really stiffen when they got into our territory. We just wanted to keep it up."

Griffin had 89 yards at the half. Both he and Bell would find the running much more difficult in the final 30 minutes.

Michigan received the ball to start the second half, and Bell was tackled for a loss by DeCree and Plank on third-and-two. Ohio State took over, after the punt, at the Wolverine 48 yard line. After two Griffin runs, Greene scrambled for 11 yards and a first down to the UM 33. The Buckeyes couldn't get another first down, though; and after another Greene run gained 7 yards, Ohio State faced a fourth-and-four at the Michigan 27.

Instead of going for the first down, Woody decided to go with the red hot Klaban. Once again, the walk-on kicker came through as he blasted a 45-yard kick over the uprights.

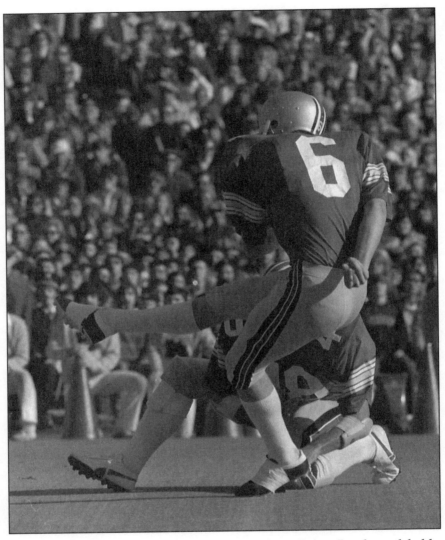

Tom Klaban kicks one of his four field goals as Brian Baschnagel holds.
PHOTO COURTESY OF BROCKWAY SPORTS PHOTOS.

"It was just one of those days when I was in 'The Zone,'" Klaban recalls. "I felt like I could have kicked a 65-yarder if it was needed. The adrenalin gets flowing, and once you have some success, your confidence just feeds off of it. It was a special feeling."

The Buckeyes now led for the first time in the game 12-10.

After forcing a Michigan punt, Ohio State gained a first down on a Brian Baschnagel wingback counter. But two plays later, Pete Johnson was stripped of the ball by Dave Brown. Tim Davis recovered for Michigan.

The teams traded punts on the next few series as the defenses began to take control. Late in the third quarter, the Wolverines looked to get excellent field position as Ohio State punter Tom Skladany would be kicking from his end zone. But Skladany blasted a 63-yard punt that was caught by Dave Brown at the UM 30. Ray Griffin had great coverage on the kick and tackled Brown at the Michigan 37 yard line.

This was a huge shift in field position as the fourth quarter got underway. It paid off for the Buckeyes several plays later when Franklin lofted a pass toward the sideline for Jim Smith that was picked off by Neal Colzie at the OSU 39. Ohio State couldn't move, though, so Skladany again got off another sledgehammer punt. This one went 51 yards and put Michigan back at their own 13 yard line.

The Wolverines put together a very good drive that carried them into Ohio State territory. Bell, who would finish with 108 yards rushing, was replaced with a fresh Rob Lytle at the tailback spot. Fullback Chuck Heater carried the ball four times, and Franklin hit two passes to put the ball at the Buckeye 39. But Michigan could get no closer as Pete Cusick tackled Franklin for a 5-yard loss on an option play and then pressured him into an incompletion on third down. Lantry was called on to try a 59-yard field goal, but it fell short.

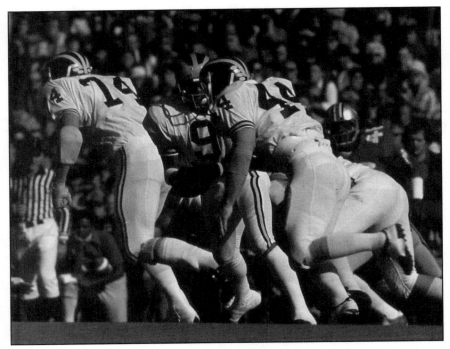

Guard Kirk Lewis leads the way as Dennis Franklin hands off to Chuck Heater in the fourth quarter. PHOTO COURTESY OF BROCKWAY SPORTS PHOTOS.

After another Ohio State punt, Michigan got the ball back with just over three minutes left in the game. Cusick again came up big for the Buckeyes by forcing an incomplete pass by Franklin on second down and, along with Buonamici and Arnie Jones, sacked him on the following play. John Anderson's punt rolled to the Ohio State 25 as all eleven Buckeyes stayed near the line of scrimmage in case of a fake.

With only 1:59 remaining in the game, Ohio State could run out the clock if they could get a first down. But the Michigan defense held and forced the Buckeyes' punt. Using their timeouts wisely, the Wolverines got the ball back at their own 47 yard line with 57 seconds left.

"We knew this was it," Dennis Franklin recalls. "This drive would determine our season."

On first down, Franklin fired a pass to Jim Smith on a post route to the Ohio State 32. This play put them in field goal range, but the Michigan offense had to get closer to give Lantry a good shot at making the winning kick. After Franklin fired an incompletion to stop the clock, Lytle then ripped off a 10-yard run up the middle for another first down at the Ohio State 22 yard line. Lytle carried the ball again and sliced for 6 more yards to put the ball at the OSU 16 with only 18 seconds left.

Michigan took their final timeout to set up Lantry's 33-yard field goal attempt.

Second chances can be rare in sports. And only a precious few have had the opportunity that Mike Lantry was faced with in 1974. After missing two long field goals at the end of the 1973 game, here he was again with everything on the line. This kick wouldn't be the difference between a win and a tie as in the previous year. It was for everything!

The Rose Bowl and a shot at a national championship would hinge on his left foot. It didn't seem right for so much pressure to be placed on a college student for two straight years. But Lantry had served a tour of duty in Vietnam, so he had already faced much more serious challenges in his young life.

The snap was good and Tom Drake spotted the football perfectly. As everyone in Ohio Stadium stood breathlessly, Lantry's foot smashed into the ball and the kick cleared the leaping Ohio State defenders at the line of scrimmage. The kick was extremely high and had more than enough distance. As the kick sailed for the left upright, time seemed to stand still.

"I really hit it well," Lantry remembers. "That may have hurt because I got a lot of height on it and it went way over the top of the uprights."

The kick passed over the top of the left upright, and the officials hesitated for a moment.

Michigan players jumped into the air with their hands up, thinking that Lantry had made it. But after a few seconds (that seemed like an eternity), the officials waved their arms signaling the kick was no good.

As the crowd rushed onto the field to celebrate with the Buckeyes, several Michigan players turned to the referees and pleaded that the kick was good.

Everyone in the stadium was on his or her feet as Lantry attempted the decisive field goal. Photo Courtesy of the Ohio State University Photo Archives.

"I was blocking on the wing. I had a perfect view of the kick," Rob Lytle recalls. "And there was no question that it was good."

Gary Moeller agrees. "That kick was good. I went out onto the hash mark after he kicked it and watched it sail inside the goal post."

After trying to block the kick, defensive end Van DeCree turned around to watch the kick. "I couldn't tell if it was good or not, so I just watched the official. When he signaled no good, I just wanted to collapse from excitement."

Some Ohio State players couldn't bear to watch.

"I thought he would make it, so I couldn't stand to watch," Tom Klaban remembers.

Archie Griffin also looked away. "I was on the sideline praying that he wouldn't make it."

Once again, Mike Lantry had to face the prospect of what might have been. "I really thought it was good. It went inside the left upright. But that's just the way it is. I was devastated. The whole team was devastated. That was the last play of my college career. Unfortunately, that is my legacy at Michigan. People don't remember the kicks I made to win games. They just remember the kicks against Ohio State."

Bo Schembechler doesn't blame Lantry for the kick. "We made enough mistakes in that game that it shouldn't have come down to a kick. We shouldn't have put him in that position."

After the field was cleared of fans and some semblance of order was restored, the Ohio State offense came onto the field to run off the final 16 seconds of the game. Cornelius Greene took a knee on the final snap, and that was it.

The Buckeyes had come from a 10-0 first quarter deficit to win the game 12-10. "We were delirious," Brian Baschnagel recalls. "You leave everything you have out on the field, and then it comes down to a kick. It was an amazing game."

In the post-game locker room celebration, Woody Hayes awarded punter Tom Skladany and placekicker Tom Klaban with game balls. "That was the greatest exhibition of kicking I ever saw!" Hayes exclaimed. "Bo said last week that the game might be decided by the kicking game, and he was right."

A game ball wasn't the only thing Klaban received after the game. Woody also awarded the walk-on kicker a full scholarship.

The win was especially sweet for Hayes. After coming back from his heart attack in the spring and overcoming the devastating loss at Michigan State, this victory was very satisfying.

Archie Griffin also kept his streak alive by rushing for a game-high 111 yards.

The loss was a painful one for the Wolverines.

"We gave every ounce of energy we had to winning, and to have it come down to that was terrible," Gil Chapman remembers.

Dennis Franklin has similar memories. "It hurt then and it hurts now. That kick sure looked good from where I was standing, but they said it missed. So we were 30-2-1 in my career and never played in a bowl game. That's ridiculous."

Michigan defensive back Dave Brown still can't believe Michigan lost the game. "Even after all these years, it bothers me. We didn't let them score a touchdown and we lost. That sticks with you."

Mike Lantry had a surprise waiting for him when he got home that night. "There was a pile of Western Union telegrams for me. A lot of them were from Ohio State fans who said they were glad they won the game, but they thought the kick was good."

While Michigan sat home for another year, Ohio State faced USC in the Rose Bowl for a shot at a national championship. The game went back and forth. With only a few minutes remaining, the Buckeyes led 17-10. But a late Trojan touchdown, followed by a two-point conversion, gave Ohio State a heartbreaking 18-17 loss.

Coincidentally, on the last play of the game, Ohio State attempted a desperation 61-yard field goal. It missed.

#4 OHIO STATE	12
#3 MICHIGAN	10

The Game 1974 — Columbus, Ohio

	Ohio State	Michigan
Total Yards	253	291
Rushing Yards	195	195
Passing Yards	58	96
First Downs	14	18
Turnovers	2	2

Key Individual Stats:

ARCHIE GRIFFIN — 25 carries, 111 yards

GORDON BELL — 25 carries, 108 yards

TOM KLABAN — 4 field goals, 47,23,43,45 yards

TOM SKLADANY — 5 punts, 42-yard average

THE GAME 1975

EVERY MICHIGAN-OHIO STATE GAME IS HUGE and carries its own unique importance. But to call the 1975 edition of "The Game" *huge* would be an understatement. For the third time in seven years, Ohio State would enter Ann Arbor ranked #1. And for the sixth straight year, Michigan would enter its clash with Ohio State undefeated. Once again, the Rose Bowl and National Championship were on the line.

Woody and Bo were both at the peak of their power. But there was one major difference between the two programs: Ohio State hadn't lost to Michigan since 1971. While that fact brought unmitigated joy to the Buckeye faithful, it brought nothing but agony and vexation to Michigan players, coaches, and fans. Both Ohio State's elation and Michigan's frustration were to reach their zenith in 1975.

For Michigan, 1975 was supposed to be a rebuilding year; but the young Wolverines grew up faster than most had anticipated. After consecutive ties to Stanford and Baylor early in the year, Michigan had cruised to seven straight wins and entered the Ohio State game ranked #4.

True freshman Rick Leach started the season at quarterback and, while still young and susceptible to mistakes, had developed into an outstanding player leading Michigan's dangerous option attack. Gordon Bell and Rob Lytle were both such great runners that Lytle was moved to fullback so he and Bell could be in the backfield at the same time. Both would finish 1975 with over 1,000 yards rushing and both would average over 5 yards per carry.

The sophomore-laden offensive line sustained a lot of injuries early in the year, but as the Ohio State game approached, they had evolved into a very solid unit. Mike Kenn, Mark Donahue, Jim Czirr, Walt Downing, and Bill Dufek paved the way for Michigan to lead the Big Ten in both rushing and total offense. But late in the year, Kenn sustained an injury and Steve King would get the start against the Buckeyes. Jim Smith and Keith Johnson were good receivers but, with a freshman quarterback and a devastating running game, Michigan rarely passed.

As the year progressed, the Michigan defense carried the team as the inexperienced offense matured. Undersized Tim Davis was the anchor of a solid defensive line that included Greg Morton and Jeff Perlinger while Calvin O'Neal led a group of fast, hard-hitting linebackers. Senior Don Dufek was the leader of a good, but young, secondary.

As usual, the defenses at the two schools ranked first and second in the Big Ten.

While Michigan's success in 1975 had been somewhat of a surprise, Ohio State was right where they were expected to be: at the top of the polls. The Buckeye seniors of 1975 were one of the best classes in Ohio State history and compared favorably to the phenomenal senior class of 1970. Archie Griffin was on his way to winning a second straight Heisman Trophy, and was the Big Ten MVP in 1973 and 1974. His backfield companion, Cornelius Greene, would win that award in 1975. Greene and Griffin combined with bruising fullback Pete Johnson to form a lethal backfield.

Archie Griffin came into the Michigan game with a streak of 31 consecutive games with over 100 yards rushing, which is a NCAA Division 1A record that still stands and might never be broken. Pete Johnson was a short yardage and goal line specialist who would finish with an amazing 25 touchdowns in 1975. All those yards and touchdowns came behind one of the best offensive lines in the country. Chris Ward, Bill Lukens, Ted Smith, Scott Dannelly, Rick Applegate, and Ron Ayers created the holes that the talented backfield exploited. Brian Baschnagel, Larry Kain, and Jim Harrell were on the receiving end of Greene's deadly play-action passes.

Just like all of Woody's great teams, this one had an amazing defense. Nick Buonamici and Bob Brudzinski both made the All-Big Ten team on the defensive line while Ed Thompson and Ken Kuhn led a very physical corps of linebackers. Tim Fox was an All-American at safety and along with Craig Cassady, Ray Griffin, and Bruce Ruhl formed a spectacular secondary. Tom Klaban and Tom Skladany, heroes of the 1974 game, were both back to handle the kicking duties.

Despite facing a difficult schedule that included Penn State and UCLA, the Buckeyes were 10-0 heading into the Michigan game with every win being by more than a touchdown.

Illinois coach Bob Blackmon called the Ohio State backfield "the greatest in the history of college football."

Cal Stoll of Minnesota agreed. "Their offense is the simplest thing to defense on the board. But try and go out there and do it on the field. The first thing you have to do is stop the buffalo (Pete Johnson), then Corny or Archie make the big play."

As always, the week of the game brought the most intense practices of the season. Freshman Rick Leach was pulled aside by some of his older teammates and told what to expect in the upcoming game.

"Some of the veteran players told me to buckle my chinstrap up a little tighter because the hitting in this game was going to be unbelievable," Leach remembers. "Man, were they right."

Both teams closed practices to the media and took great pains to completely seal off their workouts from prying eyes.

One enterprising UPI photographer decided to snap a few pictures of a Michigan practice from the balcony of a nearby building. Once spotted, Bo led a charge to the balcony where he got local police to confiscate the film until after the game. He also refused to allow UPI to attend the following day's press conference and even resigned from the UPI ratings poll. For his part, the UPI photographer would call Bo and his staff "bullies." The national press had a field day with the incident and laughed at the seeming paranoia that surrounded the preparations.

In other words, it was just a typical Michigan-Ohio State week.

Woody Hayes did his part to spice up the week as well.

Tom Skladany remembers Woody pulling one of his motivational ploys before the game at Ann Arbor. "We're sitting there eating at the hotel, and everyone is quiet and obviously nervous. Suddenly, Woody starts banging his glass with a fork and calls for the headwaiter. All the girls who were serving us were very good looking, so Woody makes them go to the back and has the cooks and dishwashers come out and bring us our food. 'Men, Bo has planted these lovely co-eds here to take your minds off the game. I'm glad we caught it.' I was laughing to myself, but I think some of the younger guys believed it. All of a sudden, people are talking and getting loose. Woody had succeeded in breaking the tension."

On Saturday, a record crowd of 105,543 packed into Michigan Stadium. Michigan athletic director Don Canham's marketing genius, paired with the success that Bo was having, finally paid off as 1975 saw Michigan start the streak of games with over 100,000 in attendance that continues to this day. Before the arrival of Canham and Bo, only games against Michigan State or Ohio State would draw capacity crowds. This success was also reflected in Bo's home record. Heading into the 1975 Ohio State contest, Michigan had won 41 consecutive home games.

The game started in a flurry as Michigan received the opening kickoff and gained one first down before being forced to punt. Ohio State took over and showed why they were the nation's top team.

On the second play of the drive, Cornelius Greene scrambled away from pressure and hit Griffin with a pass down to the Michigan 46 yard line. After three plays gained over 9 yards, the Buckeyes faced the first big play of the game with a fourth-and-inches at the UM 36.

From the full house backfield, Pete Johnson slammed in the Michigan line for three yards and a first down. Six plays later, the Buckeyes were confronted with another fourth down and less than a yard to go. Once again, Johnson drove straight up the middle for a first down. After two running plays put the ball at the 7 yard line, Ohio State faced third-and-goal.

At the snap, Greene dropped back to pass and waited for Pete Johnson to slip out of the backfield on a fullback delay. Johnson caught the pass at the 2 and bulled into the end zone for his 23rd touchdown of the year.

"That was a special play that we put in just for Michigan," offensive coach George Chaump explains.

Michigan defensive lineman Tim Davis recalls being surprised by the play. "That pass was totally new to us and we were unprepared for it. That was a great call by them."

Tom Klaban kicked the extra point, and Ohio State had taken an early 7-0 lead on their opening drive. It would be their last sustained offense until the middle of the fourth quarter.

On the next few possessions, Michigan sandwiched two punts around one for Ohio State as the defenses controlled play. After a short punt gave the Buckeyes good field position at the Michigan 43, Greene fired a deep pass that was intercepted by Jim Bolden at the UM 1 yard line. This was the first in an avalanche of turnovers that carried over into the second quarter as the defenses from both teams were playing inspired football.

After a Rob Lytle run gave the Wolverines some breathing room out to their 11 yard line, the first quarter ended.

Two plays later, Gordon Bell's elusiveness was on display as he cut back across the field on a toss play. Bell ran the power sweep to the right, broke a tackle by Cassady, and bolted left down the sideline before Ken Kuhn saved a touchdown by tackling Bell at the Ohio State 44.

The 43-yard run was wasted, though, as Bell fumbled an option pitch from Leach on the next play. Tim Fox was bearing down on Bell as he was about to take the pitch, and linebacker Ed Thompson recovered the ball at the OSU 45.

Gordon Bell breaks into the Ohio State secondary on a 43-yard run at the beginning of the second quarter. Bell would rush for over 100 yards in the first half. PHOTO COURTESY OF THE BENTLEY HISTORICAL LIBRARY, UNIVERSITY OF MICHIGAN.

On the first play after the turnover, Greene passed to tight end Larry Kain for 15 yards to the Michigan 40 yard line. This first down early in the second quarter would be the last the Buckeyes would manage until less than seven minutes remained in the game. Three plays later, Greene was forced out of the pocket by middle guard Tim Davis, a fixture in the OSU backfield all day, and threw an interception on the sideline to Don Dufek at the Michigan 25.

On the ensuing possession, Michigan drove into Ohio State territory on a 28-yard pass from Leach to Keith Johnson. But after a sack by blitzing safety Ray Griffin put the Wolverines in a third-and-long situation, Leach fired an interception that Cassady returned to the OSU 32. Ohio State couldn't move the ball, however, and were forced to punt the ball away.

Michigan again marched into Buckeye territory with runs by Lytle and a 24-yard burst by Gordon Bell. But once again, the drive was killed by a turnover. Rick Leach was hit by Ed Thompson on an option play and fumbled. Aaron Brown recovered the loose ball after several players scrambled for it, and Ohio State took over at their own 30 yard line.

"The hitting was just so fierce out there that turnovers were bound to happen," Rob Lytle recalls. "Both defenses were just teeing off on whoever had the ball."

After the tenacious Michigan defense forced another three-and-out by Ohio State, Tom Skladany drilled a long, booming punt that went all the way into the end zone. Michigan started at their 20 yard line and moved the ball down the field.

Mixing runs by Lytle and Bell with a 30-yard pass from Leach to Keith Johnson, the Wolverines drove deep into Ohio State territory. Leach then scrambled for another first down on a third-and-ten play to keep the drive alive and hit Johnson again for a first down to the OSU 11.

On the next play, Leach tossed the ball to Gordon Bell on an apparent sweep. But Bell stopped, cocked his arm, and threw a beautiful halfback pass to Jim Smith in the corner of the end zone. Craig Cassady had great coverage on the play, but the pass was right where it needed to be and Smith made a fantastic fingertip catch for a touchdown.

"We were waiting for the right time to call that play," Bo recalls. "We felt that with the success we had running the ball, we could suck the defensive backs in and throw one over their heads."

Cassady's heads-up play kept him in position to defend the pass, but the throw and catch were just right. Bob Wood kicked the extra point and with only 24 seconds left in the half, the score was tied 7-7.

Things went from bad to worse for Ohio State on the ensuing kickoff when Archie Griffin was hit by Derek Howard and fumbled. John Anderson recovered for the Wolverines at the OSU 21 yard line with 18 seconds remaining.

After two incomplete passes by Leach, Bell was given the ball on a draw play but only reached the 19. As time expired in the first half, Bob Wood was wide left on the 36-yard field goal that would have given Michigan the lead and added to their momentum.

"Not giving up any points there was big," remembers Brian Baschnagel. "Things weren't going for us already. We didn't need to be in a deeper hole."

The first half stats looked very unfamiliar for a Michigan-Ohio State contest. The teams combined to turn the ball over six times. After their opening drive, the Buckeye offense had gone nowhere. The swarming and gang-tackling Michigan defense was keying on Griffin, and he finished the first half with only 25 rushing yards. The Ohio State offense had only generated 78 yards of total offense with 63 of that coming on their first possession. Michigan had racked up 237 total yards with Bell gaining 101 on the ground. If the stellar Buckeye defense hadn't kept forcing turnovers, the score would most likely been much different than 7-7.

Michigan defensive coordinator Gary Moeller felt very confident at halftime. "After that first series, we really controlled their offense. We were all over Griffin, and our defensive line was putting a lot of pressure on Greene when they passed. If we could keep it up, we thought we'd win the game."

Archie Griffin remembers thinking that the Buckeyes just needed one big play to loosen up the Michigan defense. "They were really focusing in on me. We hoped that would open up other parts of our offense, but they did a great job of shutting us down. We knew we could come back in the second half and move the ball. We just needed to get some momentum."

The third quarter didn't bring the momentum the Ohio State offense was looking for. On the opening drive of the second half, the Buckeyes gained over nine yards on three plays. But Woody decided not to gamble on fourth down from his own 29 and punted the ball away.

Michigan took over on their own 42 and quickly moved the ball to the Ohio State 34 where they faced third-and-four. Leach ran the option to try to get the first down, but Ray Griffin blitzed into the backfield to disrupt the play while Nick Buonamici dropped Leach for a two-yard loss. On fourth down, Greg Willner was short on the 53-yard field goal attempt and Ohio State took over at their own 20.

The teams traded punts on their next few possessions. As the third quarter progressed, Michigan was slowly winning the field position battle. The Wolverines managed to get at least one first down on each drive while Ohio State went three-and-out on every possession.

Leach, Lytle, and Bell continued to get decent yardage, but the exhausted Buckeye defense always managed to stop them short of scoring territory. The Ohio State offense, on the other hand, was completely shut down by Michigan. Griffin drew two or three tacklers every time he touched the ball, and Pete Johnson and Greene fared no better.

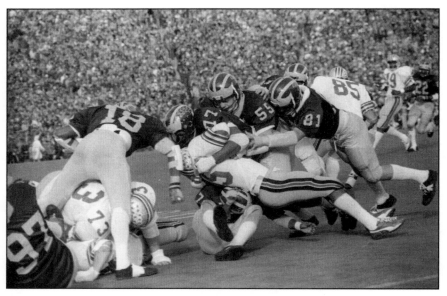

The tenacious Michigan defense swarms Archie Griffin. Griffin's streak of 31 consecutive 100-yard games would come to an end as he rushed for only 46 yards. Photo Courtesy of the Bentley Historical Library, University of Michigan.

As the third quarter came to a close, the score was still tied at 7-7.

But the overwhelming feeling was that Michigan was winning the game. After each stop by the Wolverine defense, it seemed their tired counterparts on the Ohio State defense would finally crack after spending almost the entire second and third quarters on the field. The proud Buckeye defense refused to give in, though, and they were keeping Ohio State's hopes of a victory alive.

At the beginning of the fourth quarter, the Ohio State defense again stopped what had been a promising Michigan drive that reached Buckeye territory. The field position battle had finally paid off for the Wolverines as John Anderson's punt rolled to the Ohio State 6 yard line.

In the shadow of their own goal posts, the Buckeyes tried to give themselves some breathing room. But just as in the previous seven drives by Ohio State, the Michigan defense rose to the occasion.

On first down, Ohio State ran a toss sweep right with Griffin. Defensive lineman Jeff Perlinger fought through a block to drop Griffin for a loss of three yards back to the 3. On second down, Pete Johnson rammed into the middle of the line but was stacked up after only gaining a yard. Woody decided to play it safe this close to his end zone and called for a punt on third down. Skladany didn't hit one of his better punts, and Michigan took over at the OSU 43.

After two running plays only netted one yard, the Wolverines faced a third-and-nine situation. Leach threw an incomplete pass on third down, but Aaron Brown was penalized for being offsides and Michigan was given a second chance. On the following play, Leach pitched to Bell on an option and the senior tailback gained just enough to get the first down. Leach then hit Jim Smith with a 9-yard pass, and Lytle ran for 11 more yards to the OSU 13. Two plays later, Leach hit a diving Smith with an 11-yard completion down to the 4 yard line. After getting 3 yards on first-and-goal, Leach then ran an option play into the end zone for a touchdown and a 13-7 Michigan lead.

The Michigan Stadium crowd went crazy, and Bob Wood nailed the extra point to make the score 14-7 with 7:11 remaining in the game.

The Buckeyes were now behind by a touchdown. They hadn't gained a first down since there were over 13 minutes left in the second quarter, and they were in a hostile stadium facing a supercharged defense that had controlled them for most of the game. They were 80 yards away from the end zone and they knew that if they couldn't get anything going, their defense was probably going to collapse. It was literally "now or never" for Ohio State.

When the Buckeye offense took the field, Cornelius Greene took charge in the huddle.

Archie Griffin remembers what was said: "Cornelius just said, 'Hey guys, let's say a prayer to ask the Lord to give us strength,' so we all held hands and that's what we did. We didn't ask to win the game. We just asked for strength."

The Buckeyes had to wait a few plays for their answer.

On first down, Greene passed deep to a double-covered Baschnagel, but the pass was badly overthrown. On second down, the Michigan defense nearly delivered the knockout blow. Greene dropped back to pass, and Tim Davis fired right into the backfield after him. Davis chased Greene all the way back to the end zone and almost sacked him for a safety. Greene was barely able to escape Davis, and now Mike Holmes and Greg Morton were bearing down on him. Just before being decked, Greene heaved a pass over the middle. The ball sailed right into the middle of a pack of players near the 30 yard line. Linebacker Calvin O'Neal had his hands on it, but it went through his grasp and four other Wolverines had a chance for the interception before the ball finally fell incomplete.

"I think about that play all the time," recalls Davis. "Had I dove at Greene at the goal line, I might have sacked him. Then I looked up and saw the ball go to O'Neal, and I thought we had it. If we get a safety or an interception there, that's the ball game. But we didn't."

Now facing third-and-ten, the Buckeyes had to have a first down. The play chosen was "84 Barb." It called for Brian Baschnagel to line up in the slot and run a flag route towards the sideline. Greene dropped back and finally had good pass protection. He fired the pass to Baschnagel who caught the ball at the 30 yard line and raced for 7 more yards before being belted down by Dwight Hicks. It was Ohio State's first first down in over two quarters, and it seemed to awaken the long dormant Buckeye offense.

That play was the turning point.

Now the Buckeyes seemed almost unstoppable. After the Baschnagel reception, Greene hit split end Lenny Willis for 14 yards to the Michigan 49. Greene continued to be hot as he again hit Willis, this time for 18 yards to the UM 31. Archie Griffin then had his best run of the day by going off right tackle for 11 yards and another first down. On the next play, Greene rolled left before taking off on a 12-yard scamper to the Michigan 8 yard line. After their long first-down drought, Ohio State now had gained one on each of their previous five plays.

With a first-and-goal at the 8, it was time to get into the full house backfield and pound the ball right at Michigan. On first down, Pete Johnson rammed off a tackle, carrying one defender and running over another for six yards down to the 2. Johnson then went up the middle for a gain of one before being stopped short of the goal line by O'Neal and Davis. On third down, Johnson was stuffed at the half-yard line by Davis, Hicks, and Jilek.

Now the ball was 18 inches from the end zone, and the Buckeyes faced fourth-and-goal. With only about 3:30 left, if Michigan could somehow hold for one more play, they could possibly run out the clock.

Greene barked out signals and then handed off to Pete Johnson for the fourth straight time, and the huge fullback blasted into the end zone for a touchdown. Tom Klaban kicked the extra point and with 3:18 remaining in the game, the score was tied again . . . at 14-14.

Everything had shifted into Ohio State's favor. The pressure was now on Michigan because a tie would send Ohio State to

Pasadena due to the Wolverines' two ties early in the season. The Buckeye defense had gotten a much-needed rest, and they were fired up as the momentum had swung to Ohio State.

Knowing they needed to score, the Michigan offense came out passing. On first down, Leach dropped back to pass and was smothered immediately by Aaron Brown and Bob Brudzinski for a nine-yard sack. Leach then lofted a pass down the left sideline for Jim Smith, but Craig Cassady had great coverage and knocked it away. On third-and-nineteen, Leach dropped back and fired a pass deep over the middle for Smith.

The ball was overthrown and picked off by Ray Griffin at the Michigan 33. He raced down the sideline before finally being knocked out of bounds at the 3 yard line by Leach.

Griffin was mobbed by his teammates as the Ohio State bench and the few thousand Buckeye fans in the stands went wild.

Ray Griffin's interception return set up the winning touchdown. PHOTO COURTESY OF BROCKWAY SPORTS PHOTOS.

On the very next play, Pete Johnson barreled into the end zone for his third touchdown of the day. Klaban again kicked the extra point and now, unbelievably, Ohio State had a 21-14 lead with 2:19 left in the game.

As the Buckeyes celebrated, the Wolverines and their fans were in disbelief. After being dominated for over two quarters, Ohio State had scored 14 points in 59 seconds.

The crowd that just a few minutes before had been in pandemonium now sat stunned.

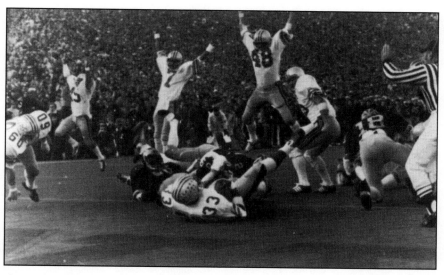

Griffin, Greene, and Baschnagel signal touchdown as Pete Johnson plows into the end zone for the winning score. PHOTO COURTESY OF THE OHIO STATE UNIVERSITY PHOTO ARCHIVES.

Michigan now needed a touchdown and a two-point conversion to win. Leach scrambled for two yards on first down before throwing two incompletions to set up fourth-and-eight from the 22. On fourth down, Leach threw deep for Jim Smith, but Craig Cassady stepped in front of him and got his second interception of the game. Cassady returned the pick to the Michigan 30 and now Ohio State could run out the clock.

Pete Johnson carried four straight times for 19 yards as the clock wound down. On the final play of the game, Cornelius Greene took a knee and with that, the game was over.

The Buckeye players hoisted Woody Hayes on their shoulders, and someone handed him a bouquet of roses for the victory ride. As the Ohio State team and fans celebrated, the Michigan players walked toward the locker room wondering just what they had to do to beat Ohio State again.

"That loss really, really hurt and it still does," remembers Michigan assistant Jerry Hanlon. "We controlled the game, but let it slip away. That was very frustrating."

Bo Schembechler agrees. "That was another one of those games where we won all the stats, and they won the game. There is no satisfaction in that. If anything, that adds to the pain."

Woody Hayes, holding roses, is given a victory ride at Michigan Stadium.
PHOTO COURTESY OF BROCKWAY SPORTS PHOTOS.

Gordon Bell and Rob Lytle both rushed for over 100 yards while Griffin's record streak came to an end as he only gained 46 yards. But Archie Griffin was thrilled that his brother Ray had played an integral part in the victory.

"Winning was always much more important to me than the rushing records, so I was elated. And the fact that my brother set up the winning touchdown made it even more special. The Griffin house was jumping that night."

Woody Hayes was so overjoyed with the come-from-behind win that his post-game press conference turned into passionate, rambling monologue that referred to the JFK assassination, the course of the nation, and his outburst at Ann Arbor in 1971.

Woody reminded the gathered reporters that it was the anniversary of the Kennedy assassination. "I have to believe that in this nation, from that day forward, we've been on the skids. I think we started doubting one another and doubting our abilities. All this stuff about a major plot causing the death of our great President is not true, but it did create a lot of doubters. But I'll tell you something: That Michigan team didn't doubt one another and this great Ohio State team didn't doubt one another, or we couldn't have won."

As the stunned reporters stood listening, Woody kept going. "But we better turn it around, because we're sure going the wrong way."

Hayes then expressed some regret about his actions during the 1971 game at Ann Arbor. ". . . I worry about the thing I did here four years ago. It didn't hurt anybody, but it was the sort of thing that could inflame and that's the reason I'd think again before ever doing it again."

With that, the press conference was over as the media members sat and looked around at each other in disbelief.

"That was Woody," Bo explains. "He wasn't like everyone else, and you never knew what to expect out of him. That's what made him great."

For the first time in Big Ten history, a team played in a bowl other than the Rose. Michigan lost in the Orange Bowl to eventual national champion Oklahoma 14-6. That national championship was made possible by the shocking upset that occurred just a few hours before in the Rose Bowl.

Ohio State had defeated UCLA at Los Angeles earlier in the year by a score of 41-20. But the Bruins stunned the Buckeyes 23-10 in their Rose Bowl rematch. After beating Michigan, everyone assumed that Ohio State would again roll over UCLA and win the national title. But the inspired Bruins overcame a 3-0 halftime deficit to pull the upset.

It has been widely speculated that had Ohio State won that game, Woody Hayes would have retired. That would have given him a fourth national title and sent him out on top with one of his favorite classes.

But it wasn't meant to be.

Regardless of the bowls, the 1975 game remains one of the great wins in Ohio State history, and the players who came in during the 1972 season never lost to the Wolverines.

The 1975 game was also yet another bitter pill for Michigan to swallow. Four years in a row, they played lights-out football against the Buckeyes and four years in a row, they failed to defeat them. The frustration levels had reached an all-time high.

But the tables were set to turn once again.

#1 OHIO STATE	21
#4 MICHIGAN	14

The Game 1975 — Ann Arbor, Michigan

	Ohio State	Michigan
Total Yards	188	361
Rushing Yards	124	248
Passing Yards	64	113
First Downs	12	19
Turnovers	3	5

Key Individual Stats:

GORDON BELL — 21 carries, 124 yards

ROB LYTLE — 18 carries, 104 yards

PETE JOHNSON — 3 touchdowns

THE GAME
1976

WHEN SO MUCH EMPHASIS is put on winning a single game, failing to win that game can be excruciating. And going four years without winning that game is almost unbearable. Despite gaining more yards and getting more first downs for four straight years, Michigan was unable to beat the Buckeyes.

Ohio State had a strangle hold on the Rose Bowl from 1972-1975, and it would be hard to imagine how that stuck in the craw of everyone in the Michigan program. It seemed like no matter how well Michigan played, the Buckeyes managed to be better when the game was on the line.

But in 1976, the pendulum would begin to swing in the other direction.

Like Woody in 1974, Bo had spent the spring of 1976 recovering from heart surgery. Gary Moeller had guided the Wolverines through spring practice, but Bo was back at it by fall camp. His recovery was probably accelerated by the fact that the 1976 team would be one of the best teams he ever assembled. They spent most of the year ranked #1 until being upset by Purdue in early November.

The strength of the team was a big-play offense that led the nation in both points and rushing yards per game, and was first in the Big Ten in total offense. Sophomore Rick Leach was in his second year as starting quarterback and he had become a master at Michigan's tricky option-based offense. Leach combined with

Rob Lytle, Russell Davis, and Harlan Huckleby to form one of the fastest backfields in Big Ten history. Lytle was extremely versatile as he played both tailback and fullback, and entered the Ohio State game with 1,237 yards and 12 touchdowns.

Leach was an effective passer and had a good group of receivers to throw to in split ends Jim Smith and Curt Stephenson, and tight end Gene Johnson. But Michigan preferred to pound their opposition with their relentless ground game and, as always, the offensive line was the key. Mike Kenn, Gerry Szara, Walt Downing, Mark Donahue, and Bill Dufek formed one of the best lines in the country.

The Michigan defense had also made a name for themselves. They were first nationally in defense against the score by allowing only 8.1 points per game, and they recorded four shutouts. The defensive line was deep and talented as Dom Tedesco, Tom Seabron, Greg Morton, Bob Lang, Steve Graves, John Hennessy, and John Anderson rotated to keep everyone fresh. Calvin O'Neal was an All-American at linebacker, while Jim Bolden, Jim Pickens, Jerry Zuver, and Dwight Hicks formed a solid secondary.

Ohio State was a young team in 1976, especially on the offensive side of the ball where six starters were lost to graduation. Rod Gerald replaced Cornelius Greene at the quarterback position, but he went down with an injury in mid-season. Senior Jim Pacenta took his place and led the Buckeyes to four straight wins. Jeff Logan had the unenviable task of filling Archie Griffin shoes, but he did a fantastic job by rushing for over 1,100 yards. Bruising fullback Pete Johnson was back and scored 18 touchdowns to bring his career total to a staggering 53.

The offensive line had to be rebuilt but Chris Ward, Jim Savoca, Mark Lang, Bill Lukens, and Lou Pietrini jelled as the season progressed. Greg Storer and Bill Jaco held down the tight end spots while Herman Jones and Jim Harrell were the split ends. All-American punter Tom Skladany returned and also took over the place-kicking duties.

The Buckeye defense was probably stronger than they had been in 1975. After enduring several injuries early in the year, the defense rebounded to lead the Big Ten in rushing and total defense. The front seven was probably the nation's best with a good mix of experience and young talent. Bob Brudzinski, Nick Buonamici, Aaron Brown, Eddie Beamon, and Kelton Dansler were very strong and quick on the defensive line. Ed Thompson and Tom Cousineau made a great pair of linebackers while Mike Guess, Tom Roche, Joe Allegro, and Ray Griffin formed a very good secondary.

Ohio State again faced a tough non-conference schedule and after winning at Penn State, the Buckeyes were upset at home by Missouri and tied by UCLA. The young team started to mature at this point, and they reeled off six straight wins heading into the Michigan game. Ohio State had already captured at least a share of the Big Ten title and could win it outright with a win over Michigan.

This would be the first time since 1967 that both teams had a loss entering "The Game."

There seemed to be more pressure on the Wolverines during game week. They were constantly being reminded that they hadn't beaten the Buckeyes since 1971 and that they hadn't won at Columbus since 1966.

"We didn't need any reminders," Bo explains. "But we kept hearing about it. I told the players we could either go down there and do something about it, or we could listen to it for another year."

Fullback Russell Davis recalls the intensity of that week. "That was as brutal a week of practice that I've ever been involved in. We absolutely HAD to win that game, and we really banged heads in practice. My brother was on the scout team, and his job was to emulate Pete Johnson that week. I don't know how he survived it. He was getting drilled by the defense on every play."

Buckeye quarterback Jim Pacenta has similar memories about Woody's practices that week. "Like every Michigan game, we practiced harder and with more intensity than for any other game. Actually, Bill Lukens had a banged-up shoulder and probably needed to rest. I think the physical nature of those practices probably had a negative effect on him that week. But when it's Michigan week, everyone gets after it, regardless of your health."

The night before the game, Michigan defensive coordinator Gary Moeller spent some extra time talking to his players. "Ohio State was one game away from tying Oklahoma's record of 123 consecutive games without being shutout," Moeller recalls. "We specifically talked about holding them scoreless as one of our goals for the game. We knew it would be a huge challenge, but we were extremely confident in our players and our game plan."

Both teams would customarily watch a movie on Friday night to try to relax. The Buckeyes watched the John Wayne movie *The Shootist* before heading off to the seclusion of their hotel.

Russell Davis remembers Bo asking everyone to stay for a few minutes after the movie that Michigan had watched was finished. "Bo cut the lights and had the final play of the 1975 game put on the screen. We saw Ohio State take a knee and run off the field at Michigan Stadium celebrating their win. Then he cut off the film and turned the lights back on. I'll tell you this, you could have heard a pin drop in that theatre. He had made his point, and he dismissed us. He was such a great motivator. He always knew how to push your buttons."

Bo and Woody shake hands at midfield prior to the 1976 game in Columbus.
PHOTO COURTESY OF BROCKWAY SPORTS PHOTOS.

Bright, beautiful skies greeted both teams the day of the game, but the early going was anything but sunny for either offense. Both teams were extremely fired up, and it showed in the play of the defenses. Ohio State failed to get a first down on their first four possessions, and Michigan also went three-and-out the first three times they had the ball.

"It was a defensive struggle early," Michigan linebacker Calvin O'Neal recalls. "We were flying to the ball, and so was their defense."

Late in the first quarter, the Wolverines managed to put together the game's first decent drive. Rob Lytle and Russell Davis pounded the interior of the Buckeye defense, while Lytle and Rick Leach stretched the perimeter on option plays.

As the second quarter began, the drive reached the Ohio State 36 yard line where Michigan was faced with fourth-and-one. The drive ended, however, when Lytle went over left tackle but was stuffed for a loss by Ray Griffin and Bob Brudzinski.

The defenses continued to control the game as both teams traded punts on their next few possessions. With just over four minutes left in the half, Ohio State began their best drive of the game.

On third-and-three from the OSU 32, Jeff Logan took an option pitch from Pacenta and raced down the sideline for 22 yards. On the following play, Pacenta again ran the option but faked the pitch to Logan. Pacenta cut inside, broke a tackle by Jerry Zuver, and ran for 23 yards to the Michigan 23 yard line.

"We were moving the ball right before halftime," Buckeye offensive lineman Jim Savoca remembers. "We struggled for most of the first half offensively, but our option plays were hurting them on that drive. The crowd was really into it, and we were firing off the ball. We could have gone into the locker room with the lead and the momentum if we had gotten points on that possession."

Logan carried the ball three straight times to put the ball at the UM 10. There, on second down, Woody tried to surprise the Michigan defense by calling a play-action pass. Pacenta faked to Logan and dropped back to pass. Linebacker Jerry Vogele blitzed through a gap and was all over Pacenta in the backfield. In danger of being sacked, Pacenta lofted a pass towards the front of the end zone for tight end Greg Storer. Storer was double-covered, however, and the pass was intercepted by Jim Pickens for a touchback.

"The previous week I had gotten sacked in a similar situation against Minnesota, and that knocked us out of field goal range," Pacenta explains. "I was just trying to throw it away, but I didn't have enough on it. The linebacker was in my face, and I didn't get enough arm behind it."

After the game, Woody took the blame for the turnover. "That was my call . . . I just called a bad play."

Jim Pickens leaps to intercept a pass in the end zone to end Ohio State's best scoring opportunity of the game. PHOTO COURTESY OF THE OHIO STATE UNIVERSITY PHOTO ARCHIVES.

Michigan ran out the remaining minute of the first half, and the teams went into the locker room with the game a scoreless tie.

The stats reflected the score as Ohio State had 112 yards of offense at halftime and Michigan gained 109. Each team had one good drive, but only the Buckeyes had seriously threatened to score. Buckeye punter Tom Skladany was probably the biggest weapon for either side as his booming punts kept Michigan backed up. Skladany had punted six times for a 48.3 yard average in the first two quarters, and only Jim Smith's excellent returns had kept the Wolverines from starting almost every drive deep in their own territory.

"It was anyone's game at the half," Tom Cousineau explains. "They had an unbelievable offense, but we had done a great job of stopping them in the first half. We felt like we could do it again after halftime."

Jim Pacenta agrees. "Despite the interception, that drive at the end of the second quarter gave us confidence that we could move the ball. We thought we'd continue that into the third quarter, but it just didn't work out that way."

Michigan running back Rob Lytle recalls being frustrated at halftime. "We were close to breaking a few in the first half. But, to Ohio State's credit, they had always managed to stop us. But we were all extremely confident that we were going to win. We felt that if we just came out and executed our offense, we'd move the ball."

The Wolverines received the ball at their 20 to start the second half and began marching down the field. After Leach ran for 8 yards on an option play, Russell Davis pounded for a first down on a fullback plunge off right tackle. Lytle then ran for 14 yards on an option play to the left to put the ball close to midfield. Three plays later, Michigan was faced with a critical third-and-two at the Ohio State 47 yard line.

Showing his improvisational skills, Leach ran for 20 yards on a broken play. What should have been a handoff to Lytle off left tackle turned into a quarterback draw as the confusion in the Michigan backfield froze the Buckeye defense. Leach cut back to his right and scrambled for a first down at the OSU 37.

Lytle continued his assault by taking an option pitch for 11 yards, then going up the middle for 9 more. Two plays later, Ohio State jumped offsides and gave Michigan a first down on third-and-one. On the next play, Russell Davis burst up the middle for a 3-yard touchdown run that put Michigan in front.

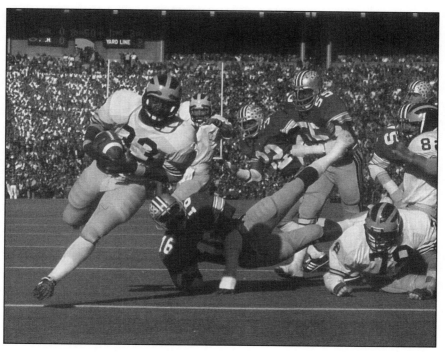

Fullback Russell Davis sprints into the end zone for the first score of the day. Photo Courtesy of Brockway Sports Photos.

Woody Hayes went ballistic on the sideline as he saw left tackle Bill Dufek move early.

"Yep, I fired out before the snap," Dufek remembers. "I was moving sideways to block inside, and that's why the linesman didn't see it. But Woody did. He was yelling at the officials that I had moved early, but they missed it. He slammed his hat down and walked off. I can still see him in my mind."

Bob Wood kicked the extra point and Michigan led 7-0.

On the ensuing possession, the Buckeye offense couldn't move the ball again and went three-and-out for the sixth time in the game. Skladany again nailed a great punt, but Jim Smith gave Michigan the ball near midfield with another good return.

The Wolverines picked up where they had left off on their previous drive. Lytle attacked the perimeter of the defense on option plays and off tackle runs while Russell Davis went up the middle on quick-hitting fullback dives.

From the Ohio State 25, Jim Smith ran for 16 yards on a well-executed wingback reverse to give Michigan a first-and-goal on the 9. After two runs gained six yards, Davis again pounded into the end zone from three yards out. Cousineau and Griffin met him at the goal line, but Davis kept his legs churning and scored his second touchdown of the day.

"It was an honor to play in that rivalry," Davis explains. "But to score two touchdowns at Columbus is a thrill that I carry with me to this day."

On the extra point attempt, holder Jerry Zuver took the snap, ran to his right, and bolted into the end zone for two points to give Michigan a 15-0 lead.

"We had worked on that all week," Bo recalls. "We had considered using it after the first touchdown, but we decided to wait until we really thought we could catch them unprepared. We didn't want to be in a position where the game could come down to a tie, so we went for it. Our sideline went nuts when we got it."

There was a sense of urgency when the Ohio State offense took the field. Down 15-0, the Buckeyes knew they had to move the ball to get back in the game and to give their beleaguered defense a rest.

After John Hennessy dropped him for a loss on first down, Jim Pacenta ran for 15 yards on an option play. Pacenta continued to be under heavy pressure whenever he went back to pass. The Buckeye quarterback then scrambled away from another sack to hit Jim Harrell over the middle for 17 yards to the OSU 48.

Defensive lineman Greg Morton kept up the heat on Pacenta by sacking him for a 7-yard loss and pressuring him on the play after that. But Pacenta again escaped the rush and hit Jeff Logan on the sideline for 16 yards on the final play of the third quarter.

Pete Johnson converted the first down by ramming forward for two yards, but Michigan was penalized for being in the neutral zone anyway so the five-yard penalty gave the Buckeyes the ball at the UM 38.

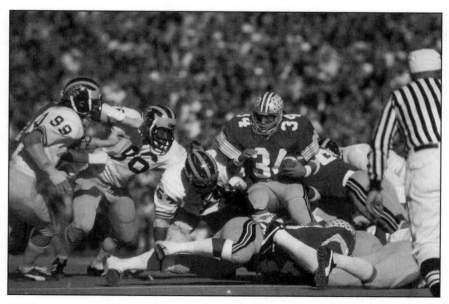

Jeff Logan attempts to spin away from the Michigan defense. Photo Courtesy of Brockway Sports Photos.

The drive came to a screeching halt on the following play when Logan fumbled an option pitch that was recovered by defensive end Tom Seabron. Michigan took over at their own 42 yard line and put together another crunching, ball-control drive. Mixing bruising runs up the middle with option plays to the outside, the Wolverines methodically moved the ball deep into Ohio State territory.

"By this time in the game, their defense was gassed," Rob Lytle explains. "They had spent almost the entire day on the field, and they were just tired. The holes were just a little bit wider, and the pursuit was just a little slower. But they never quit. They played as hard late in the game as they did in the first quarter. That's a tribute to the pride their players and coaches had. That's what makes the rivalry so special because we felt the same way."

Ten straight running plays put the ball at the OSU 16 where Michigan faced a third-and-six. Rick Leach dropped back and fired a pass for Gene Johnson, but Tom Roche cut in front of Johnson to intercept the pass at the 13 yard line.

The reprieve for the Buckeye defense was short-lived, however, as Jim Pacenta fired his own interception on the following play. Jerry Zuver picked off Pacenta's pass at the OSU 28 and returned it to the 15.

From there, Michigan continued their ground assault. Lytle went through a huge hole up the middle for 11 yards and, two plays later, Lytle shot up the middle for a touchdown. Bob Wood kicked the extra point to put Michigan ahead with a commanding 22-0 lead.

"Rob Lytle literally put our offense on his back and carried us to victory," Rick Leach recalls. "He was relentless. He'd race outside on option plays and fought for tough yards up the middle. He had a phenomenal game that day."

With the game basically over, many in Ohio Stadium began to file out.

But the Buckeye offense kept fighting. Pacenta hit Pete Johnson for 13 yards and Jim Harrell for 26 more to move the ball into Michigan territory. But sacks by John Hennessy and Jerry Meter on one play and Greg Morton and Steve Graves on another killed the drive, and Ohio State was forced to punt with under four minutes remaining.

From their 20 yard line, the Wolverines wanted to get a few first downs and run out the clock. The versatile Rob Lytle moved to fullback and ran for twice, for 14 and 4 yards, before being removed from the game. Lytle had one of the great performances in the history of the rivalry by rushing for 165 yards on 29 carries.

Rob Lytle finds running room on the outside. Lytle played both tailback and fullback, and seemed to get stronger as the game wore on. PHOTO COURTESY OF THE OHIO STATE UNIVERSITY PHOTO ARCHIVES.

Bo pulled his starters, one by one, as he wanted reserve players to get the chance to see action in the game. Harlan Huckleby used his speed to rush for 40 yards on four straight runs. As the clock continued to wind down, Stacy Johnson came in to replace Leach at quarterback, and Ralph Clayton took over at tailback. On the final play of the game, fullback Kevin King gained one yard up the middle as the clock struck zero.

The Michigan sideline celebrated wildly as they carried Schembechler off on their shoulders.

"That was just such a satisfying win," Gary Moeller explains. "After those heart-breaking losses and that tie, it felt like a huge weight had been lifted off our shoulders. I was so proud of those players. To go down to Columbus and shut out a Woody Hayes' team was an incredible accomplishment."

Michigan offensive line coach Jerry Hanlon has similar memories. "Rob Lytle had a great game, and I can't think of anyone who deserved it more. That guy did whatever you asked of him and did it well. When we needed help at fullback, he gladly switched to fullback and was very effective. No one personified what you want in a team captain any more than Lytle."

Michigan ground out 366 yards on the ground while quarterback Rick Leach was 0-6 passing. "We didn't have any passing yards, but we didn't need them," Hanlon explains. "Once we got the lead, we just kept pounding the ball at them. They had a great defense, but I think we wore them down. They were on the field all day."

The Wolverine celebration lasted onto the flight home. Bill Dufek remembers Michigan radio broadcaster Bob Ufer entertaining everyone on the plane. "He had this little coffin that he put on a stewardess' cart and was wheeling it up and down the aisles," Dufek recalls with a laugh. "It was supposed to symbolize the fact that we buried Woody, and we were all just so happy that we got a kick out of it. Ufer was always doing crazy stuff like that."

At his post game press conference, Woody Hayes graciously praised Michigan and his former assistant. "Michigan will get my vote as the number one team in the country. Any team that beats us as soundly as they did deserves to be number one. Bo should be the coach of the year after coming back from open heart surgery in the spring."

After spending four consecutive years at the Rose Bowl, Ohio State headed to Miami to take on Big 8 Champion Colorado in the Orange Bowl. After falling behind 10-0, the Buckeyes rallied to win convincingly 27-10 and finished the season ranked #6.

Michigan, on the other hand, lost a tight, defensive game in Pasadena to USC 14-6. The Trojan defense managed to shut down Michigan's vaunted ground game, and the Wolverines didn't have the passing attack to fall back on. Even with the loss, Michigan finished #3 in the final AP poll.

Bo still remembers the feeling of relief the 1976 game brought the Michigan program. "You have to understand how frustrating the previous four years had been to understand how special that game was. After all those heartbreaks, to win 22-0 down there was very gratifying. I'll never forget it."

#4 MICHIGAN	22
#8 OHIO STATE	0

The Game 1976 — Columbus, Ohio

	Michigan	Ohio State
Total Yards	366	173
Rushing Yards	366	104
Passing Yards	0	69
First Downs	23	10

Key Individual Stats:

ROB LYTLE — 29 carries, 165 yards, 1TD

RUSSELL DAVIS — 24 carries, 83 yards, 2TD

TOM SKLADANY — 8 punts, 52.2-yard avg.

THE GAME
1977

As Michigan had learned the hard way from 1972-1975, the team that has the better statistics doesn't always win. Moving the ball up and down the field is irrelevant if you don't score points when you have the opportunity. In 1977, the Buckeyes would understand this all too well.

In fact, this game was very similar to the one in 1972, except with the roles reversed. It was another classic that would come down to the final moments to be decided. And, once again, Woody Hayes' famous sideline temper would add to the excitement.

The Wolverines were loaded again coming off their Rose Bowl season of 1976. The offense, even with the graduation of Rob Lytle and Jim Smith, was still very talented. Junior quarterback Rick Leach was in his third year as a starter and was one of the best in the country. His passing skills had improved greatly and he had plenty of weapons in split end Rick White, wingback Ralph Clayton, and tight ends Gene Johnson and Mark Schmerge.

The backfield was a good blend of speed and power with fullback Russell Davis, and tailbacks Harlan Huckleby and Roosevelt Smith. The offensive line was deep, experienced, and physical. Tackle Bill Dufek was lost for the year due to injury, but the other four starters from the previous season were back. Mike Kenn, Walt Downing, and Mark Donahue each made the All-Big Ten team, while Greg Bartnick, Gerry Szara, John Powers, and Jon Geisler took turns in the starting line-up.

Michigan's defense was again one of the better units in college football. The Wolverines were fourth in the country in scoring defense and near the top in rushing defense. Dale Keitz, Steve Graves, Curtis Greer, Dom Tedesco, and All-American John Anderson made up a strong defensive line that controlled the line of scrimmage. Ron Simpkins, Jerry Meter, and Mel Owens were the linebackers while Dwight Hicks, Derek Howard, Mike Jolly, and Jim Pickens formed one of the nation's best secondaries.

A week after destroying fifth-ranked Texas A&M 41-3 in a non-conference game, Michigan moved into the top spot in the polls. But Minnesota shocked the Wolverines 16-0 in late October. Michigan rebounded to win three straight games and entered "The Game" 9-1 and ranked #5.

Ohio State had put together an even better season. The Buckeye offense was led by the lightning-quick Rod Gerald, and the junior quarterback was the key to an explosive option attack. With the emergence of Ron Springs at tailback, senior Jeff Logan played both fullback and tailback. This gave Ohio State one of their fastest backfields ever. Springs amassed over 1,000 yards rushing. And when Logan missed several games to injury, bruising fullbacks Paul Campbell and Joel Payton picked up the slack.

What made the Buckeye running game so dangerous was the quickness, strength, and timing of an outstanding offensive line. All-American Chris Ward teamed with Mark Lang, Ernie Andria, Ken Fritz, Tim Vogler, and Joe Robinson to open holes for the skilled players. When defenses threw everything into slowing down the ferocious ground game, Jim Harrell, Herman Jones, Jimmie Moore, and Greg Storer would burn them with receptions on play-action passes.

While the Ohio State offense was racking up yardage, the defense was suffocating the opposition. They recorded four shutouts and held four other opponents to a touchdown or less to lead the country in defense against the score. Aaron Brown, Byron Cato, Luther Henson, Paul Ross, and Eddie Beamon were solid up front while All-American Tom Cousineau and Dave Adkins formed an excellent linebacking corps. The secondary of Ray Griffin, Joe Allegro, Mike Guess, Leonard Mills, and Tom Roche was experienced, fast, and was very physical.

Only an onsides kick and last-second field goal in a loss to Oklahoma kept the Buckeyes from being ranked #1. After the loss to the Sooners, Ohio State reeled off seven wins and were never seriously challenged as they clinched at least a share of their record seventh consecutive Big Ten Championship. The fourth-ranked Buckeyes could capture the title outright by winning at Ann Arbor.

Injuries in the backfield became a concern for Michigan the week of the game. Starting tailback Harlan Huckleby was nursing a tender hamstring and his back-up, Roosevelt Smith, wasn't completely healthy either. But in a game of this magnitude, no one who could walk would sit out.

Bo was also worried about defending the speed of the Ohio State offense. "Rod Gerald was a fantastic option quarterback," Bo recalls. "You let him get to the outside with backs like Logan and Springs, and you're in trouble. You can't prepare for his quickness because you can't simulate that kind of elusiveness in practice. We knew we had to contain him and make him physically pay the price whenever he ran the ball."

As usual, both teams were sky high the day of the game. And the fireworks began even before the opening kickoff. The NCAA record crowd of 106,024 saw the Buckeyes run out the tunnel and head for the Go Blue banner, just as they had in 1973.

This time, however, the Michigan students holding the banner held their ground and a scuffle ensued. For a few moments, there were pushing and shoving as emotions were running high, and Woody was right in the middle of it. Finally, order was restored as the Buckeyes ran to their bench with their smiling coach leading the way.

The millions watching on television missed this altercation and the first seven minutes of the game. ABC was covering the historic visit to Israel by Egyptian President Anwar Sadat and joined the game in progress during the opening drive of the game. ABC affiliates received thousands of angry phone calls from viewers who were livid about missing even a single play of the game.

The Buckeyes received the opening kickoff and came charging out of the gate. Using option plays to Ron Springs and a few quarterback runs by Rod Gerald, the Ohio State offense marched deep into Michigan territory. Gerald scrambled for one first down and passed to Springs for another as the Wolverine defense was having trouble adjusting to the speed of the Buckeye option attack.

"Those guys were lethal on the outside," Michigan defensive back Mike Jolly explains. "You had to execute your assignment or you were in trouble. Gerald was as quick as anyone I ever played against, and they had all those fast backs that he could pitch the ball to. If someone missed a tackle or blew an assignment, it was six points."

In what would become the story of the game, the Michigan defense tightened up as the Buckeyes neared their goal line.

On third-and-three from the Wolverine 11, defensive lineman Dale Keitz chopped down fullback Paul Campbell for no gain. Keitz fought off a block and took Campbell's feet out from under him, or he would have gotten a first down. Vlade

Janakievski came in and kicked a 29-yard field goal to give Ohio State an early 3-0 lead.

After Michigan went three-and-out on their first possession, the Buckeye offense went right back to work. Gerald again hit Springs for a first down and continued to pick up very good yardage on option keepers. After Gerald gained 10 and 12 yards on consecutive option plays, Jeff Logan switched from fullback to tailback and hit the corner for a first down to the Michigan 11 yard line.

The Michigan defense spent most of the first quarter chasing the elusive Ron Gerald. Photo Courtesy of the Ohio State University Photo Archives.

Once again, the Wolverine defense stiffened as Ohio State drove towards the end zone.

Gerald was forced out of the pocket by Keitz and sacked back at the UM 17 by Curtis Greer on second down. Following a five-yard procedure penalty, Gerald then pitched poorly on an option play and Bill Jaco recovered for the Buckeyes at the 25 yard line. The loss of yardage on these plays was critical as Janakievski was wide left on a 42-yard field goal.

Despite completely dominating the first quarter, Ohio State led only 3-0.

As the second quarter began, Michigan put together a good drive that flipped field position and kept the dangerous Buckeye offense on the sideline. Leach converted a third-and-eight play by hitting Ralph Clayton on a 22-yard post pattern. Russell Davis and Harlan Huckleby found some running room up the middle, and Leach gained another first down by connecting with Doug Marsh for eight yards on third-and-six. The drive stalled, however, and Greg Wilner missed a 47-yard field goal that would have tied the game.

The teams traded punts on their next few possessions as the Michigan defense finally had some success slowing down the Ohio State option game. Field position slowly started to favor Michigan following the exchange of punts, and the Wolverines took over at the OSU 46.

After strong runs by fullback Russell Davis and tailback Roosevelt Smith moved the ball to the 30 yard line, Michigan was faced with third-and-eleven.

"We needed that first down," Rick Leach remembers. "They knew we'd be passing, but we thought we might be able to sneak Roosevelt Smith out of the backfield."

The play worked perfectly. Leach dropped back and looked downfield as Smith ran to the right and circled out of the backfield without any defender following him. Leach kept his eyes downfield to draw the defense away from Smith before lofting a pass to him at the 18 yard line. Smith caught the ball in stride and raced to the OSU 8 before being upended by Mike Guess.

Russell Davis pounded up the middle on consecutive carries to gain seven yards to set up a third-and-goal from the 1 yard line. Roosevelt Smith then finished the drive by plunging into the end zone as the Michigan Stadium crowd roared their approval. Greg Wilner nailed the extra point as the Wolverines took a 7-3 lead with 1:20 left in the first half.

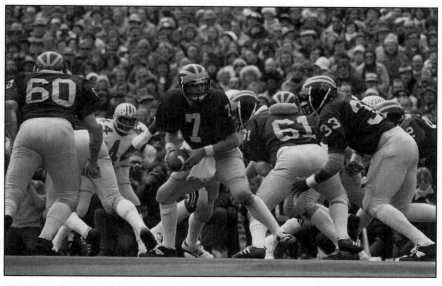

Rick Leach hands off to Russell Davis. PHOTO COURTESY OF BROCKWAY SPORTS PHOTOS.

Ohio State used the remaining time to quickly get into field goal position. Two Logan carries moved the ball to the OSU 42. Then Gerald continued to be hot by hitting Springs for 14 yards and Herman Jones for 14 more. With only ten seconds left, Vlade Janakievski missed a 49-yard field goal to keep the halftime score 7-3.

The Buckeye offense had generated 17 first downs in the half and had a large advantage in total yards. But, as Michigan in 1972, they couldn't capitalize on their scoring opportunities.

"We were really moving the ball well," Jeff Logan explains. "Everything seemed to be working until we got close. We were running the ball very well, and Gerald was hurting them with his passing. But once we got inside the 20, we'd either make a mistake or they would make a great defensive play. You can't squander scoring opportunities in a Michigan game. But we thought that we'd punch a few over in the second half. We were very confident after the way we'd moved the ball."

Michigan received the ball to start the third quarter and gained one first down on a 12-yard scramble by Leach before being forced to punt. John Anderson got off a great kick that pinned Ohio State back at their 16 yard line.

On the first play, Ron Springs ran up the middle and was hit hard by Steve Graves. The ball popped loose and was snatched out of the air by Michigan linebacker Ron Simpkins at the OSU 20.

"That was a huge play for us," defensive lineman Curtis Greer remembers. "One of our goals as a defense was to give our offense a short field. Getting the Ohio State offense off the field was also important because they were so dangerous."

The Wolverines didn't waste the opportunity.

Rick Leach got 11 yards on an option play to the left to give Michigan a first-and-goal from the 9 yard line. From there, fullback Russell Davis followed guard Mark Donahue on a trap play for six yards to the OSU 3. Davis then rammed into the center of the line to put the ball at the 2.

On third down, Leach took the snap, faked a handoff to Davis, and ran down the line to the left. Buckeye linebacker Tom

Cousineau hit Leach at the 1 yard line, but he was able to extend the ball across the goal line for a touchdown.

As toilet paper streamed down on the field from the delirious student section, Greg Wilner kicked his second extra point of the game to give Michigan a 14-3 lead.

Despite being behind, the Ohio State offense continued with the game plan that had been successful in the first half. Springs took an option pitch for six yards and a sweep for eight more before Gerald hit tight end Bill Jaco for 14 yards down the sideline. Gerald again showed off his passing skills by throwing deep to split end Jim Harrell for a 33-yard completion to the UM 25.

"Rod Gerald was excellent that day," offensive assistant George Chaump remembers. "He had always been a great option quarterback but during that game, he also was deadly throwing the ball. It puts a ton of pressure on a defense when they have to be so careful to defend the option, yet still worry about having to watch for the pass."

Runs by Gerald, Springs, and Campbell gave the Buckeyes another first down at the Michigan 12 yard line. But, for the third time in the game, Ohio State would penetrate inside the UM 15 but would be unable to finish the drive with a touchdown.

It wouldn't be the last.

Three straight great defensive plays by Curtis Greer, Mike Jolly, and Ron Simpkins pushed the Buckeyes back to the Michigan 27. From there, Janakievski kicked a 44-yard field goal that cut the Wolverine lead to 14-6 with under six minutes left in the third quarter.

Two plays after the ensuing kickoff, Ohio State would get the ball right back.

Roosevelt Smith ran off right tackle where he was belted by linebacker Dave Adkins and fumbled. Joe Allegro pounced on the ball for the Buckeyes at the UM 31 and, just like that, Ohio State was in scoring position again.

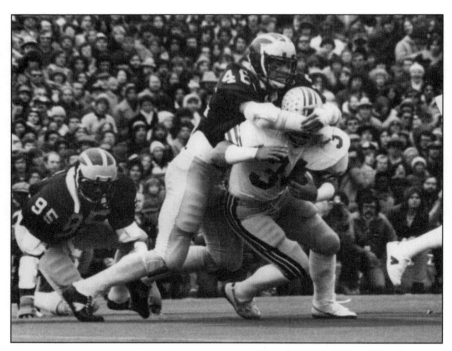

The 1977 game was one of the most physical in the series. Here, Jerry Meter wraps up Jeff Logan. PHOTO COURTESY OF THE BENTLEY HISTORICAL LIBRARY, UNIVERSITY OF MICHIGAN.

Once again, however, the Michigan defense rose to the occasion when threatened. Jeff Logan carried twice for a total of nine yards to set up third-and-one from the 22 yard line. Woody put the offense into the full house backfield and called on his fullback, Paul Campbell, to ram into the line for the first down. But Ron Simpkins shot through a gap over left guard to drop Campbell for a loss of two yards. The play became even more costly for Ohio State when Janakievski was wide left on the 42-yard field goal attempt.

Michigan was unable to move the ball on their next possession and would again have to punt to Ohio State.

Rick Leach recalls how difficult it was to move against the Buckeye defense. "We struggled against their defense that day.

We didn't really have a lot success moving the ball on them the entire game, but we were fortunate enough to get yards when it counted. They had great players on that defense. Tom Cousineau was probably the best defensive player I ever faced. He was all over the field making tackles."

As Roosevelt Smith takes the handoff, linebacker Tom Cousineau closes the hole. PHOTO COURTESY OF THE BENTLEY HISTORICAL LIBRARY, UNIVERSITY OF MICHIGAN.

When the Buckeyes got the ball back, they started another deep drive into Michigan territory. Springs took an option pitch for 17 yards for one first down, then caught a 10-yard pass from Gerald for another as the fourth quarter began. Ohio State moved the ball to the Wolverine 10 yard line where they were faced with a fourth-and-one.

After threatening to score so many times, it seemed almost inevitable that the Buckeyes would finally push one into the end zone. ABC analyst Ara Parseghian said, "You just get the feeling that Ohio State is going to score. They just keep knocking at the door."

On fourth down, Woody again chose to run Campbell up the middle from the full house backfield. This time, defensive lineman Steve Graves plugged the middle and Campbell was met at the line of scrimmage by linebacker Mel Owens. Campbell spun away from Owens but was hit immediately by Simpkins and Anderson. The chains were brought in to measure, and the ball was just inches short of the first down.

The Wolverine defense stormed off the field to a wild ovation from the Michigan Stadium crowd.

On their ensuing possession, the Michigan offense put together a good drive that took some time off the clock and moved the ball out of their end of the field. Using option runs by Leach and power runs up the middle by Davis and Smith, the Wolverines drove into Buckeye territory before having the drive stall.

Anderson again pinned Ohio State deep as the Buckeyes took over at their own 10 yard line with 8:10 left in the game.

Gerald was again brilliant. After two plays gained five yards, Gerald converted the crucial first down by hitting Harrell over the middle for 21 yards to the OSU 36. Gerald then passed to Springs for nine yards and scrambled up the middle on a quarterback draw for 16 more. Springs and Campbell then combined for nine yards on two carries to set up third-and-one at the UM 25.

Instead of hammering into the center of the line again, Woody called for a toss play to Springs. Springs took the pitch to the right, followed a great block by Campbell, broke a tackle by Jim Pickens at the 23, and raced down the sideline to the Michigan 8 yard line.

With another first-and-goal situation, Ohio State seemed destined to finally score a touchdown. A touchdown and two-point conversion would tie the game. And since the Buckeyes had already clinched a share of the championship, a tie would send Ohio State to the Rose Bowl.

On first down, Gerald brought his team to the line. Woody called for an option play to the short side of the field because he thought John Anderson, Michigan's best defensive end, would be to the wide side. But he wasn't. Gerald took the snap, faked a handoff to Logan, and slid down the line. Anderson blew past Logan and hit Gerald just as he was pitching out to Springs.

"I showed that I was going to take the fullback," Anderson explains. "But instead, I went after Gerald. I was lucky enough to catch him just as he was releasing the pitch, and the ball flew about 10 yards into the backfield."

The hit sent the ball bouncing backwards, and Springs slid to the turf as he tried to stop his momentum. Michigan defensive back Derek Howard jumped on the ball at the 18 yard line to kill the Ohio State drive.

As the crowd went crazy and the Michigan defense flew off the field, ABC cameraman Mike Freeman was on the Ohio State sideline catching Woody Hayes' reaction to the turnover. Woody grimaced in anger and disgust before he slammed his phone onto the ground. Woody then realized that his frustration was being filmed. He ran two or three steps to get to Freeman and took a swing at the cameraman. Freeman managed to block most of the blow, but the entire incident was captured on TV.

Woody Hayes slams down his phone following Gerald's fumble late in the fourth quarter. Seconds later, Hayes would take a swing at ABC cameraman Mike Freeman.

185

With only 3:58 remaining in the game, Michigan needed to get a few first downs to kill the clock. But the Buckeye defense forced a three-and-out and used a timeout to stop the clock and get the ball back for their offense. After the punt, Ohio State had the ball at their own 35 with 2:10 left.

The game would come down to this final drive.

On the first play, Gerald scrambled up the middle for 12 yards to put the ball at the OSU 47. Springs then caught a pass out of the backfield for three yards, and Gerald threw an incomplete pass deep to Harrell. On third down, Gerald again hit Springs out of the back field but for only a four-yard gain. With 1:10 left in the game and facing fourth-and-three, Ohio State called a timeout to stop the clock and discuss their options.

Woody called for a toss play to Springs to the short side of the field, the same play that had gained a key first down on the previous drive. But this time, John Anderson took on the blocks of tight end Jimmy Moore and fullback Paul Campbell to stretch the play to the sideline. This allowed Derek Howard and Ron Simpkins to meet Springs at the corner and force him out of bounds short of the first down.

The Michigan defense had held again. That sealed it.

As the Michigan bench erupted in celebration, the crowd again cheered the play of the defense. Rick Leach fell on the ball three times to run out the remainder of the clock. As it hit 00:00, the Wolverine players hoisted Bo on their shoulders and carried him across the field. The fans poured onto the field to celebrate with the players as the tunnel into the locker room turned into a mass of humanity.

Rick Leach summed up the game well. "Ohio State had a great game plan, and they outplayed us," Leach remembers. "But our defense won that game. Ohio State kept moving the ball and threatened to score, but our defense kept stopping them. It was a magnificent performance by the defense."

Bo concurs. "That was a game we might very well have lost. But our defense was just tenacious. It felt great because there had been games where we had all the statistics and they had the points. But this time, it was reversed. That was satisfying."

Frustration was probably the best way to describe how the Buckeyes felt. Offensive lineman Ernie Andria explains what the players were thinking. "It was frustrating to move the ball up and down the field, and come up short in the red zone. We blew some things ourselves, but you have to take your hat off to their defense as well."

In his post-game press conference, Woody Hayes summed up his feeling on the game by saying: "This is, by far, the best game we ever played and lost."

The Buckeyes led in every statistic except the final score. The had more first downs, more passing yards, more rushing yards, and more time of possession. They had penetrated the Michigan 15 yard line on five different possessions and only came away with two paltry field goals. That was the story of the game.

Woody was also asked about the incident with Mike Freeman. He asked the reporter how he would like it if someone was always sticking a microphone in his face. Woody then abruptly ended the press conference and walked away.

Hayes was blasted in the media for his latest outburst but, at first, refused to apologize. The Tuesday after the game, Woody brought up the incident again at the team's annual awards banquet. With his voice booming, Woody said that he was tired of a camera shoved in his face. But he did soften his previous stance and showed regret for the altercation. "I'm sorry for what I did, sure. Do I make mistakes? Sure, I make lots of them. Everybody here knows I make mistakes. We all do. Now, as far as I'm concerned, that thing's all over."

Michigan would go on to lose the Rose Bowl to underdog Washington 27-20 and finish the season ranked #9. It was Michigan's fourth Rose Bowl loss under Bo. Ohio State didn't recover from the loss and was blasted by Alabama in the Sugar Bowl 35-6. Many players feel that the loss at Michigan took so much out of them that they didn't regain their focus for the Sugar Bowl.

After going four years without a victory, Michigan had now won two straight and kept the Buckeyes out of the end zone in both games. Bo and Woody were now 4-4-1 in their nine meetings and each had tasted glorious victories and bitter, heartbreaking defeats.

Though no one knew it at the time, the Ten Year War was nearing its conclusion.

#5 MICHIGAN	14
#4 OHIO STATE	6

The Game 1977 — Ann Arbor, Michigan

	Michigan	Ohio State
Total Yards	196	352
Rushing Yards	141	208
Passing Yards	55	144
First Downs	10	23

Key Individual Stats:

ROD GERALD — 13-16-144, 52 rushing yards

RUSSELL DAVIS — 17 carries, 56 yards

ROOSEVELT SMITH — 11 carries, 46 yards, 1TD

THE GAME
1978

LIKE MOST OF THEIR GAMES AGAINST EACH OTHER, the 1978 clash between Bo and Woody proved to be a defensive contest. And for the third game in a row, it was the Michigan defense that prevailed. The Wolverines had experienced total frustration from 1972-1975, and now it would be the Buckeyes' turn.

Unfortunately, this would be the final battle between the two giants, Bo and Woody.

Ohio State was a team in transition in 1978, and they experienced a fair share of peaks and valleys. Art Schlichter was one of the most widely heralded recruits in Ohio history, and both Bo and Woody had coveted Schlichter during the recruiting process. Woody won the battle by promising Schlichter the starting job his freshman year, something Bo wouldn't do with Rick Leach coming back.

Woody was true to his word and replaced Rod Gerald with Schlichter from the opening snap of the season. While the option would still be a big part of the offense with Schlichter, Woody had decided to move towards more of a passing game. And with Schlichter's talent, the move would pay off for Ohio State down the road.

While the freshman quarterback was getting his feet wet, the Buckeye offense turned to a powerful ground game. Senior Ron Springs was back at the tailback spot, but injuries sidelined him for parts of the season. Ricky Johnson and Calvin Murray replaced Springs when he was hurt, and they performed well. The fullback position was well stocked with Paul Campbell, Joel Payton, and Ric Volley all getting plenty of carries.

The offensive line saw several different rotations as injuries forced the coaches to juggle the lineup. Joe Robinson, Ernie Andria, Jim Savoca, Tim Vogler, Ken Fritz, and Keith Ferguson formed the nucleus of a solid offensive line. Tight ends Jimmy Moore and Bill Jaco and receivers Rod Gerald and Doug Donley were talented and gave Schlichter several good targets.

Gerald, the starting quarterback in 1976 and 1977, had moved to split end to make way for Schlichter and to enhance his future in the NFL. Gerald still took snaps under center and played occasionally at quarterback.

The Buckeye defense struggled early in the year, especially against passing teams, but had improved as the season progressed. Byron Cato, Mark Sullivan, Luther Henson, Paul Ross, Kelton Dansler, Al Washington, and All-American Tom Cousineau made up a pretty good front seven. Cousineau was the best defensive player in the nation and carried on the long tradition of great Ohio State linebackers.

The secondary was young and consisted of Todd Bell, Vince Skillings, Rob Murphy, and Mike Guess. They were very talented, but their inexperience showed early in the year. By the time of the Michigan game, they had solidified into a good unit.

After starting the year 2-2-1, with losses to Penn State and Purdue and a tie with SMU, the Buckeyes rebounded to win five straight games. If they could beat Michigan, they would clinch a share of a seventh consecutive Big Ten title and go to the Rose Bowl.

Woody had done a very good job of salvaging a young team that could have crumbled after their early season struggles.

Michigan, on the other hand, had again put together another outstanding season. Senior quarterback Rick Leach was a legitimate Heisman candidate and had set the NCAA record for touchdowns accounted for. Over his four years as starting quarterback, his passing skills had steadily improved to the point where he was as dangerous throwing the ball as he was running the option. This improvement was partially due to the talent Michigan had at tight end and receiver. Gene Johnson, Doug Marsh, Ralph Clayton, and Rodney Feaster gave Leach many talented weapons to throw to.

The running game was still the trademark of the Michigan offense, and they used several different backs to wear down the opposition. Harlan Huckleby, Roosevelt Smith, Butch Woolfolk, and Stanley Edwards gave the Wolverines a deep rotation at tailback while senior Russell Davis returned for his third season as starting fullback. The offensive line was shuffled often due to injuries but Jon Giesler, Steve Nauta, Bill Dufek, John Powers, Greg Bartnick, John Arbeznik, and Mike Leoni gave Michigan one of the better lines in the country.

Michigan's defense was again one of the nation's best. They led the Big Ten in rushing, total, and scoring defense and had recorded four shutouts on the year. Chris Godfrey, Dale Keitz, Mike Trgovac, and Curtis Greer were solid up front while Tom Seabron, Ron Simpkins, and Andy Cannavino made up a physical linebacking corps. The secondary of Mike Jolly, Mike Harden, Mark Braman, and Gene Bell was fast and talented.

The Wolverines started the year 4-0, including a win over Notre Dame at South Bend, before losing at home to Michigan State. Michigan then reeled off five wins in a row to come into the Ohio State game at 9-1 and ranked #6 nationally. The winner would tie Michigan State for the conference championship and would head to Pasadena. The Spartans were on probation for recruiting violations and were prohibited from post- season play. The loser would head to the Gator Bowl to face Clemson.

Both teams had been forced to fight through injuries all season long.

The week of the game, Michigan's depth in the backfield would be tested. Starting tailback Harlan Huckleby wouldn't play due to a knee injury, and Roosevelt Smith and Russell Davis both missed practice time. Ohio State had similar problems along their offensive line. Tackle Joe Robinson had been banged up but would play, and guards Ernie Andria and Jim Savoca would rotate throughout the game.

Woody was always nervous about practice security the week of the game, and he took extreme measures to insure that no one would spy on his team's workouts.

"Woody put huge tarps across the closed end of the stadium while we were practicing to make sure no one could see inside," Tom Cousineau remembers. "He would also position some team managers with binoculars outside the stadium to look at the windows of the dorm towers to make sure that we weren't being spied on from there. He took the Michigan game very seriously, and so did the players."

Almost every game between Bo and Woody set new attendance records, and 1978 was no exception. A crowd of 88,358 packed into Ohio Stadium to witness yet another battle for the Rose Bowl. The crowd was loud and rowdy, and the Buckeyes responded to that by controlling the first several minutes of play.

The Wolverines received the ball to start the game and gained two first downs on runs by Leach and freshman Butch Woolfolk, who started at tailback. But the drive came to a halt when Leach was sacked on third-and-eight by Kelton Dansler.

Ohio State took over at their own 27 and promptly started moving the ball. Using option plays and fullback plunges up the middle, the Buckeyes drove into Michigan territory.

Schlichter and Springs had success on the outside, and fullbacks Ric Volley and Paul Campbell converted three third-and-short plays. After moving as deep as the Michigan 23 yard line, Schlichter was thrown for a six-yard loss and Bob Atha was wide left on a 38-yard field goal attempt.

The Ohio State defense then forced a three-and-out by Michigan.

Defensive lineman Luther Henson remembers bottling up the Wolverine offense early in the game. "We were flying to the ball and controlling the line of scrimmage. They were trying to get outside but our pursuit was cutting them off, and we were getting pressure on Leach when they passed."

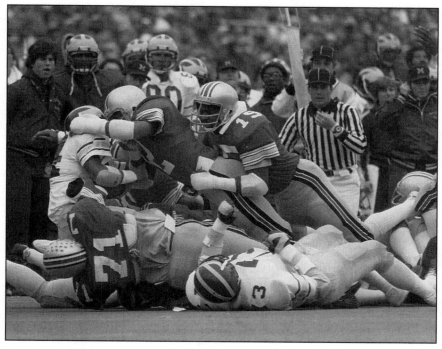

Butch Woolfolk ran into a very strong Ohio State defense early in the game.
PHOTO COURTESY OF BROCKWAY SPORTS PHOTOS.

After the Michigan punt, the Buckeyes got the ball back at midfield. Ric Volley put Ohio State back into scoring territory by breaking a run up the middle for 21 yards, then Ron Springs hit the left corner on an option pitch for 11 more.

"We were knocking them off the ball early," offensive lineman Ernie Andria recalls. "Our option stuff was hurting them on the outside, and we were able to make room for the fullback up the middle."

From there, the Michigan defense tightened up and Bob Atha came in to kick a 29-yard field goal to give Ohio State a 3-0 lead.

After the OSU field goal, Leach came out firing. On their first two drives, the Wolverine offense hadn't attempted a pass.

"We wanted to establish the run right off the bat," Bo explains. "But their defense was fired up, and we weren't getting the holes we needed to move the ball. We knew we were going to have to loosen them up throwing the ball before our ground game would be effective."

After Woolfolk was stuffed again on first down, Leach went to work. Using play-action to freeze the linebackers, Leach connected on three straight passes. The first was a throw to tight end Doug Marsh for 26 yards down the sideline. Marsh had gotten behind the linebackers and Leach lofted a pass over their heads to Marsh. On the next play, Leach again faked a handoff before hitting Woolfolk over the middle for 14 yards to the Ohio State 30 yard line.

On the following play, the call was for an option, but Leach noticed that cornerback Todd Bell was coming on a blitz. "I saw their defensive back showing blitz," Leach remembers. "I knew that would give Rodney Feaster one-on-one coverage on a post pattern so I audibled out of the option. I got good protection and the play worked beautifully."

Leach ran the play-action fake, fullback Russell Davis picked up Bell on the blitz, and Leach fired a perfect strike towards Feaster. Mike Guess had decent coverage, but Feaster had beaten him slightly to the inside. The pass was right where it needed to be as Feaster caught it at the 8 yard line and ran into the end zone without breaking stride. Greg Willner added the extra point and Michigan took the lead at 7-3.

As the second quarter began, the teams traded punts on their next few possessions. Butch Woolfolk injured a leg and had to be replaced with Roosevelt Smith who wasn't completely healthy himself. Rick Leach was also hurt as he pulled a hamstring on an option keeper. Although his mobility was limited, Leach refused to leave the game.

Bo Schembechler and Rick Leach discuss their options on the sideline. Despite a pulled hamstring, Leach stayed in the game. PHOTO COURTESY OF THE OHIO STATE UNIVERSITY PHOTO ARCHIVES.

With under seven minutes left in the half, Ohio State got the ball back at their own 39 and put together what would turn out to be their last good drive of the game. Springs and Schlichter had success on the flanks of the Michigan defense as the option propelled the Buckeyes into scoring territory.

"I remember getting pinned inside on an option play to Springs," defensive back Mike Jolly explains with a laugh. "My job was to keep the play inside, but I tried to run around the blocker and got pushed out of position. As Springs was running downfield, I could hear Bo screaming at me."

But at the UM 24, Schlichter dropped back to pass and was blindsided by blitzing linebacker Jerry Meter. The ball popped loose and was recovered by Michigan's Andy Cannavino to kill the promising drive.

There was 3:20 left in the second period after the turnover, and the Wolverines went right to work.

Roosevelt Smith ran through a huge hole off left tackle for 16 yards on the first play and Leach hit Ralph Clayton for 15 more, over the middle, three plays later. Facing a third-and-one at the OSU 14, Leach again went to the air. The Ohio State defense was expecting a run to pick up the first down, and Leach used play-action to capitalize on that. Leach faked a handoff and hit tight end Gene Johnson at the 2 yard line. As Johnson turned to go into the end zone, defensive back Vince Skillings hit Johnson from behind and stripped him of the ball just short of the goal line.

The ball bounced into the end zone where it was recovered by Skillings for a touchback.

The big defensive play by Skillings had taken a touchdown away from Michigan and gave momentum to the Buckeyes as both teams headed for the locker room.

"That gave us a boost right before halftime," Tom Cousineau recalls. "That saved a touchdown and kept the score 7-3. We felt that we had done a pretty good job of defending them in the first half and that we'd continue to for the rest of the game."

In the Michigan locker room, Rick Leach informed Bo that his hamstring was still a problem and that he was having trouble moving. Leach explains that he wasn't going to sit out. "I told Bo that I was hurting and my mobility would be limited. He asked me if I could still play, and I said yes. There was no way I was taking myself out of this game. Unless I just couldn't do the job, I was playing."

Bo remembers making some adjustments. "It limited us in regards to running the option, but we still ran most of our offense. We called for more power runs and pitches to keep Leach from running any more than he had to, but that was about it. Leach was a warrior. He would have played through anything."

The second half, just as in the 1976 game also at Columbus, would belong to Michigan. Ohio State simply couldn't move the ball against the Michigan defense. The option plays to the outside that had been successful in the first two quarters were completely cut off, and the Wolverines controlled the line of scrimmage.

"We had a lot of confidence in our schemes and our coaching," defensive lineman Curtis Greer explains. "We took away the option and then their isolation play. That put the pressure on their passing game to move the ball. That obviously wasn't their strength, and it was too much to ask of a freshman quarterback."

Mike Jolly brings down Ron Springs. The Ohio State running game was ineffective against the Michigan defense after halftime. PHOTO COURTESY OF BROCKWAY SPORTS PHOTOS.

On Michigan's second possession of the third quarter, they again moved deep into Ohio State territory. Roosevelt Smith was finding running room off tackle and on counter plays while fullback Lawrence Reid pounded inside on quick-hitting traps. Leach hit tight end Doug Marsh for 13 yards on one pass play, then executed a perfect screen pass to Reid for 11 more to the OSU 8. Two plays later, Michigan faced third-and-goal from the 11 yard line after a penalty.

If the Buckeyes could hold and force a field goal, they would still only be down by one score.

Leach dropped back to pass, rolled left to get away from the pressure, and drew the defense to him. As the defenders ran towards him, Leach dropped a pass over their heads to Roosevelt

Smith at the 7. Smith outran linebacker Al Washington to the end zone to put Michigan ahead 13-3.

As the Wolverines celebrated in the end zone, they caught a glimpse of something funny on the Ohio State sideline.

"We looked over and saw Woody Hayes punching himself in the face," Rick Leach remembers. "He was literally punching himself square in the face. We obviously got a big kick out of that."

Television replays would show Woody landing three hard right hands to his head.

After Willner kicked the extra point, Michigan's lead was 14-3 with just over four minutes left in the third quarter. It wasn't time for Ohio State to panic, but they needed to at least get a few first downs to help out their field position situation. But once again, the Buckeyes punted after three plays.

Michigan took over at their own 22 and again gained good yardage on the ground as the fourth quarter got underway. Smith, Davis, and Woolfolk continued to rip off decent gains as the Wolverines moved to the OSU 34. The Buckeyes stiffened there and forced a punt, which was downed at the 1 yard line.

With 11:52 left in the game and his offense struggling and pinned deep, Woody decided to make a change at quarterback. Rod Gerald was inserted into the line-up to try to turn things around.

Jim Savoca recalls the challenge that Gerald was facing. "Our offense was based on timing, and you don't just turn that on and off. Gerald was one of the greatest option quarterbacks ever, but not after barely playing that position all year."

Gerald fared no better than Schlichter as the Buckeye offense again failed to gain a first down. Michigan got the ball back at the OSU 42 and ate up another few minutes off the clock.

Roosevelt Smith was the workhorse as he carried three more times before having to leave the game with a twisted knee. The drive eventually stalled and Greg Willner's 43-yard field goal attempt was wide to the left.

The score remained 14-3 with 7:16 remaining.

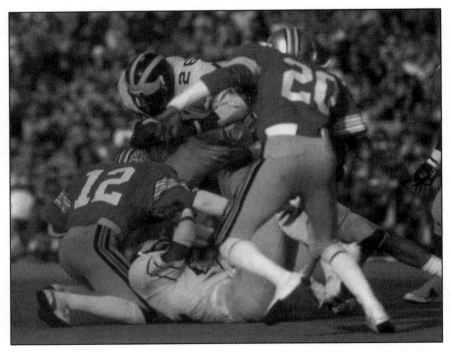

Roosevelt Smith twisted his knee on this carry and would not return to the game. Photo Courtesy of Brockway Sports Photos.

Gerald stayed in at quarterback for the next series, but the Michigan defense again shut the Buckeyes down. Woody decided to gamble on fourth-and-five from the OSU 31 and called for a fake punt. Joel Payton tried to run right for the first down but was tackled for no gain.

With the game in hand and Leach hobbled, Bo replaced him with B.J. Dickey. Michigan was unable to convert on fourth-

and-five from the Ohio State 26, and the Buckeyes took over with 3:44 left in the game.

Schlichter was back in at quarterback, and he immediately hit Gerald with a 25-yard pass over the middle for the only Buckeye first down of the second half. The success was short-lived as Schlichter threw an interception to Mike Jolly two plays later to give Michigan the ball at the UM 48.

Michigan punted after three plays and the Buckeyes had one final chance when they got the ball back at their own 5 yard line with 1:36 left.

No miracle was forthcoming as this drive ended without a first down four plays later. B.J. Dickey downed the ball on the final play of the game to give Michigan its third straight win over the Buckeyes.

"Winning three in a row felt so good," Russell Davis explains. "And with two of those wins coming at Columbus, that made it even more special."

Rick Leach has similar memories. "That win really kind of put a stamp on our four years at Michigan. And to do it at Ohio State just made it more satisfying."

Almost 30 years later, Bo is effusive in his praise for Leach. "No one knew how bad he was hurting in that second half. But he stayed in the game and even threw a beautiful touchdown pass. He was just a great player with a great attitude."

Woody was subdued in his post-game press conference. He praised Michigan and said, "We weren't quite good enough to win."

After several more questions, a Chicago reporter who Woody didn't care for asked him if he was aware that his team hadn't scored a touchdown against the Wolverines in three years. "I'm aware of that and you're the guy who would mention it," Woody said angrily.

Michigan went on to lose, again, in the Rose Bowl to national champion USC 17-10 and finished the year ranked #5. Ohio State would play a fateful game against Clemson. Late in the game, Clemson linebacker Charlie Bauman intercepted a Schlichter pass to seal the game.

After Baumann was knocked out of bounds near the Ohio State bench, Woody Hayes spun Baumann around and hit him under the facemask. Buckeye players immediately pulled Woody away from Baumann, but the damage had been done.

Woody was fired the next morning.

The Ten Year War was over.

#6 MICHIGAN	14
#16 OHIO STATE	3

The Game 1978 — Columbus, Ohio

	Michigan	Ohio State
Total Yards	364	216
Rushing Yards	198	168
Passing Yards	166	48
First Downs	21	11

Key Individual Stats:

RICK LEACH — 11-21-166-2TD

ROOSEVELT SMITH — 10 carries, 67 yards

BUTCH WOOLFOLK — 15 carries, 41 yards

RUSSELL DAVIS — 13 carries, 48 yards

Epilogue

A T THE END OF THEIR TEN GAMES AGAINST EACH OTHER, Bo had won five, Woody had won four, and one game ended in a tie. Both teams made five trips to the Rose Bowl, and each team had won or shared eight Big Ten titles.

Woody Hayes had always preached that when you're knocked down, you get back up. And that's precisely what Woody did after being fired for punching a Clemson player in the Gator Bowl. He stayed at Ohio State as a professor emeritus and continued to work with those who needed his help. If the university initiated a fund drive, Woody would help raise money. If his former players needed a job, Woody would move heaven and earth to help them get it. The stories of his generosity to anyone who needed help are legendary. That was the private side of Woody Hayes that he didn't want anyone to see.

Bo Schembechler continued to coach at Michigan through the 1989 season before his retirement. His teams would capture another five Big Ten championships in his tenure. Today, Bo still maintains an office at the Michigan football complex and gives much of the same support that Woody did after his coaching career.

"After I left the NFL, I came back to see Bo," Russell Davis recalls. "I told him I wanted to finish my degree and he immediately got on the phone. In ten minutes, he had me registered, he had me assigned to an advisor, and he even lined up a place for my family and me to stay. He didn't owe me anything. He just did it because that's the kind of man he is."

The values that Woody and Bo instilled in the men who came through their programs echo to this day. Hard work, integrity, honesty, and commitment are lessons that their players have taken with them throughout their lives.

"Woody Hayes taught me how to win," Luther Henson explains. "But, more importantly than that, he taught me how to prepare to win."

Tim Davis uses similar words to describe what he learned from Bo. "The man taught us about life. He showed us how to work, how to treat people, and how to react to adversity. We're better people because of him."

These values also affected the rivalry. As intense and bitterly contested as the games were, the one word that is used most often to describe the opposing program was "respect."

"I consider it an honor to say that I played in those games," Rick Leach explains. "We wanted to beat Ohio State in the worst way, but we just had so much *respect* for them."

Archie Griffin feels the same way. "Players go to Ohio State and to Michigan to play in that game. There is a mutual *respect* there that makes the rivalry something special. Coach Hayes and Coach Schembechler certainly made sure of that."

Each year, as the Michigan-Ohio State game approaches, Bo is frequently asked about his battles with Woody. "Every time I give an interview about those games, it always makes me miss Woody because he'd get so much enjoyment out of reminiscing about those games. I loved competing against him and he loved competing against me. For ten years, we had the most gut-wrenching, nerve-racking, rivalry anywhere. It was beautiful."

It certainly was.

A portion of the proceeds from this book will go to the Woody and Anne Hayes 1968 National Championship Athletic Scholarship Fund at Ohio State and the Millie Schembechler Adrenal Cancer Research Fund at Michigan. To donate separately to these funds, please use the following contact information:

The Woody and Anne Hayes 1968 National Championship Scholarship Fund
Project Fund 603023
Call 614-688-4501
http://www.giveto.osu.edu/

The Millie Schembechler Adrenal Cancer Research Fund
Call 734-764-2592
http://www.cancer.med.umich.edu/